Panache
at Rose Hill

A Celebration of the Joy of Cooking
Including Traditional Southern Recipes

Montgomery, Alabama

PANACHE AT ROSE HILL

Additional copies may be obtained at the cost of $14.95, plus $3.00 postage and handling, each book. Alabama residents add $.90 sales tax, each book.

Send to:

Panache at Rose Hill
11250 Hwy. 80, E
Montgomery, Alabama 36117

ISBN : 0-9658397-0-2

First Printing, May, 1996
Second Printing, June, 1997

Printed in the USA by

WIMMER

The Wimmer Companies

Memphis

HISTORY OF THE RESTAURANT: PANACHE AT ROSE HILL

Barbara Duke and Shirley Sandy had a blind date. Since both were in the food business, they shared a mutual wholesaler.

Each was experiencing difficulties with their present businesses involving lease agreements. Knowing this, their wholesaler played cupid and gave Barbara Shirley's telephone number. Upon meeting, and in the blink of an eye, they were in business.

The first year they catered out of a small rental kitchen. They did all of the cooking, deliveries and clean-up. Their husbands were amazingly helpful on some of the larger catering jobs. Family and friends were often used as servers.

A year later, Barbara and a friend were on a Sunday drive. Barbara sighted an old southern planter's home on 25 plus acres for sale. Barbara and Shirley made an appointment to see the house and fell in love with it. A few days later they signed a contract and flew to the bank. After filling out what seemed to be thousands of forms, the Small Business Loan was approved within two weeks. Can you believe that? Dreams really can come true! And without a signature of the male gender.

Both had shared a dream of opening a restaurant in a country setting serving up-scaled southern cuisine for special events.

Many bids were taken for renovation of the house. They decided on what became a construction crew from the funny papers. Any day they expected the plumber to say, "I'll gladly pay you Tuesday for a hamburger today." He looked just like Whimpy from Popeye and plumbed like Tim Allen from the comedy series, "Home Improvement".

One horror after another happened. In the final analysis, there was no outside wall to the kitchen. The Health Department changed their minds on the final inspection and said a second septic tank would be necessary after all.

Naturally, the septic tank was not included in the original bid. The outside kitchen wall certainly was, but guess what? There was no more money except their operating capital for the first year. It was used to finish the job, and they were even short on that.

Barbara, Shirley and their husbands worked hard to save money. They scrubbed and waxed floors, pressure washed the outside of the house and washed and scraped tons of windows. Bob, Barbara's husband, and a local resident, Curtis Lockley, worked non-stop cleaning up the grounds. It was good for Bob; he lost 20 pounds while wielding a chain saw.

Business was good the first year, but their pay checks were slim or none due to the loss of their operating capital.

John, Shirley's husband, washed thousands of dishes the first two years and Bob maintained the grounds with Curtis and still does with occasional help from locals. John still gets recruited into the kitchen occasionally.

Barbara and Shirley have enjoyed a wonderful partnership. Barbara takes care of daily calls, meets potential customers to show the house and books parties. Shirley orders all the food, handles all kitchen affairs, does all of the cooking and keeps everyone in stitches with her stories about her family.

Shirley and Barbara have many funny incidents that have happened at Rose Hill. As Shirley remembers some of her favorites: "There was the time one of our new, more well-endowed, waitresses came in the kitchen proclaiming how hard it was for her to get between the tables. Then with the most serious look on her face she said, 'Will it be alright if I just hand them the plates to hand down the table?' "

"Then there was the time the power went off about three hours before a wedding reception in August, possibly the hottest time of the year in Alabama. We spent one hour on the phone begging the power company to come to our aid. Finally they pulled a line from a neighboring community after we told them the icing was running down the sides of the wedding cake. The power went on about 45 minutes before the wedding party arrived. It wasn't really cool, but at least you could breathe."

Barbara remembers: "We had a wedding in March planned, and most all of the food, even the cake, was prepared except for stacking and decorating. Wouldn't you know, it snowed on that day! It hadn't snowed in March in practically 100 years, and it snowed on this day! Well, we were the first ones to make tracks on the interstate that morning at 6:00 A.M. We had to use a flashlight to find all the food in our walk-in cooler. I literally held the wedding cake in my lap all the way to the wedding site. (Couldn't have it at Rose Hill—no power). We took everything to the bride's mother's home, and Shirley fed 50 people a wonderful brunch by noon, and that's not an easy task on a regular size stove. We even took the bloody marys. They really enjoyed those! It'll be a wedding they will tell their grandchildren about. We'll tell ours, too."

Corein McElvy, Shirley's mother, a.k.a. Dabbo and Thelma Edgar, Barbara's mother, a.k.a. Ma, have been called in on some of the "we're not going to make it days!" They have never let them down.

Panache at Rose Hill is approaching its seventh year and business is booming. This was one blind date that actually turned out. Throughout all of these years, Shirley and Barbara have only had two fights — so far. Pretty good record!

HISTORY OF PANACHE AT ROSE HILL

The original Rose Hill was built in the early 1800's by Henry Lucas, the wealthiest landowner in Alabama, and her first millionaire. Mr. Lucas owned 4,000 acres. He cultivated 40 of those acres into rose beds. In 1840 the stagecoach stopped at Rose Hill for changing horses. Our state archives tells about the ladies disembarking the carriages and wandering through extensive gardens and greenhouses during the delay. It also documents the "gentry" from Montgomery enjoying Mr. Lucas' Sunday afternoon hospitality for horse racing events.

La Fayette traveled through Montgomery in the 1820's. He spent the night in a house on Mr. Lucas' plantation during his visit. Later the house was turned into a tavern. It has been meticulously restored and has a home in "Old Alabama Town" (a Landmark's project in Montgomery) where it is known as Lucas' Tavern. Highway 80, which fronts Rose Hill, is part of the Old Federal Highway that extended to Washington, D.C.

Mr. Lucas died before the Civil War, and is buried along with his wife at Old Augusta Cemetery about three miles from the home site.

Some of his descendants have visited Panache at Rose Hill, but we have not been able to locate any pictures of the original Rose Hill except one given to us by our friend, John Scott, a local attorney and author of "Memories of the Mount," a chronicle of the history of Mt. Meigs, the community that sprung up around Rose Hill.

The house that our restaurant occupies was built in 1918 by the Relfe family. Mose Smith purchased the home in 1949 and lived here until his death eight years ago. Shirley and I bought the house and twenty-five acres from Mose's estate to establish a facility for private events. The family seems to be very pleased about this use of the house, since Mose was a great cook, and a generous and hospitable person. He especially loved to invite guests home for Sunday "dinner". The buttermilk pie recipe that we serve was given to us by the family. We have changed it somewhat and embellished it with the blackberry sauce.

We have shared many important events in the lives of our guests. It's like having a large extended family. Each event receives the same consideration, planning and attention to detail. We hope we'll see you sometime at Panache at Rose Hill, and share in the planning of your special event, or just have you enjoy a Southern dining experience and our hospitality.

Barbara and Shirley

EXCERPT FROM THE BOOK
MEMORIES OF THE MOUNT
BY
JOHN B. SCOTT, JR.

As time passed, the look of the land softened, substantial houses rose and life for all began to resemble the easier patterns of the old, established planter communities from which the pioneering settlers had come. If one had to choose an exemplar of the early planters who settled around Mt. Meigs and their rising fortunes, it would probably be Henry Lucas. Lucas was one of the many Georgians who migrated to Montgomery County after the Creek Indian War. When he arrived at Mt. Meigs, he was not just broke but considerably in debt. However, fortunes could be made in a comparatively short time by enterprising cotton growers, and Henry Lucas proved to be genius as a planter.

By the late 1840's he owned five separate plantations around Mt. Meigs and had become known as the "prince of planters." He was Alabama's first millionaire and the richest planter in the state.

Henry Lucas's empire did not last long. He had no children of his own and, upon his death in 1858, his holdings were divided among his various step-children, nephews and nieces. Rose Hill was left to a nephew, James H. Judkins, and was home to the Judkins family for many years thereafter. With the hard times that followed the War Between the States, Rose Hill and its gardens fell into a gradual decline. Finally in 1915, the main house burned to the ground.

Subsequently, a smaller house was built on the site by the Relfe family. The Relfe house has survived and is now home to an excellent restaurant known as **"Panache at Rose Hill."** Although much has changed, Henry Lucas would still find the terraces he built, the spring he used, and southern cooking that would meet the standards he set at Rose Hill during the days of its glory.

TABLE OF CONTENTS

COOKBOOK COMMITTEE

Shirley Sandy

Barbara Duke

ACKNOWLEDGMENTS

John B. Scott, Jr., "Memories of the Mount"

Billy Birchfield, cover design

Bob Duke, the best looking yard man and valet that we know

John Sandy, our original dishwasher and beer consultant

DEDICATION

This Book is dedicated to our mothers. Because of their patience in the kitchen when we were children, cooking became a joy.

Without their love and encouragement to never turn down a challenge while growing up, we would not have been able to achieve this entrepreneurial dream.

$\mathcal{B}$everages
and
$\mathcal{A}$ppetizers

Guests are greeted
by Barbara.

Parlour after the
renovation. The
antiques came from
Shirley's and
Barbara's families.
A few pieces were
purchased locally.

SUMMER TEA

64 ounces freshly brewed tea
   (medium to strong strength),
   sweetened

64 ounces pineapple juice
1 large frozen orange juice, thawed

Stir together. Pour over ice and garnish with fresh mint and orange slice. Additional sugar and pineapple juice may be added for desired taste. Makes 16 (8 ounce) servings.

ROSE HILL PUNCH

*Erin, Shirley's niece, loves this punch! When she was younger,
the punch table had to be watched when vodka was added. Be careful!
It's so good and refreshing, you might drink too much
and it **will** sneak up on you with the vodka added.*

1 gallon cranberry juice cocktail
2 large cans frozen pink lemonade
2 large cans pineapple juice

4 liters ginger ale
1 pint raspberry sherbet or sorbet

Stir first 4 ingredients. Fold in softened sherbet. Makes about 60 (6 ounce) servings.
Very good mixed with vodka.

CHAMPAGNE PUNCH

1 large can pineapple juice
2 liters ginger ale

1 bottle champagne

Stir together and serve immediately. Makes approximately 25 (6 ounce) servings.

TEQUILA TREAT

1 quart Ruby Red grapefruit juice   ½ cup grenadine, or to taste
8 ounces tequila   16 ounces club soda

Mix first three ingredients. Stir in club soda. Serve over ice. Serves 6 to 8.

ROSE HILL LEMONADE

1 quart pink lemonade   ¾ cup grenadine, or to taste
½ cup fresh lime juice   6 ounces vodka

Stir together and pour over ice. Garnish with fresh mint. Serves 6 (8 ounce) glasses.

KAHLÚA SHAKE

whipped cream   1 quart half and half
shaved chocolate   2 cups Kahlúa
1 gallon vanilla ice cream   1 quart rum

Mash ice cream and half and half together in punch bowl with a potato masher. Stir in Kahlúa and rum. Serve in punch cups topped with whipped cream and shaved chocolate. About 35 servings.

MIDNIGHT COFFEE

whipped cream
8 cups brewed coffee
1 cup Bailey's Irish Cream

2 ounces Kahlúa
6 tablespoons sugar

Brew coffee. Add Irish Cream, Kahlúa and sugar. Serve in mugs and top with cream. Serves 8.

ROSE HILL MINT JULEP

sugar
fresh mint sprigs

2 ounces good Kentucky or
Tennessee whiskey
2 tablespoons Apricot Brandy

Make syrup. Boil 4 parts sugar to 1 part water until thick. Refrigerate (good to keep on hand). Crush 1 mint sprig in a 12 ounce glass. Add 1 ounce whiskey and ¾ ounce syrup. Stir. Partially fill two glasses with ice. Add whiskey mixture and stir. Spoon Apricot Brandy on top. Garnish with candied mint or violets. Yield 2 servings.

ROSE HILL BLOODY MARY

1 large can tomato juice
2 cans beef broth
½ cup fresh lemon juice
1 tablespoon celery salt
¼ cup Worcestershire sauce

1 tablespoon horseradish sauce
1 tablespoon Tabasco sauce, or to
taste
vodka
lime

Stir all ingredients together. Add 1 jigger vodka per 6-8 ounces mix. Add squeeze of lime, and garnish with pickled okra. Note: Too much vodka bruises the drink.

HOT SPICED APPLE WINE

Barbara acquired this recipe from the Perdido Vineyards which used to be located in Perdido, Alabama. The vineyard was Alabama's first farm winery.

1 bottle sweet apple wine
½ cup water
¼ cup sugar

4 cloves
4 whole allspice
1 1-inch stick cinnamon

Combine water and sugar in saucepan and heat to boiling. Add spices and simmer 1 minute. Add wine and heat until steam rises. Do not boil!!! Serve in mugs. Makes 6 (5 ounce) servings.

SOUTHERN FEVER

2 ounces white rum
1½ ounces Rose's lime juice

chilled tonic water
lime slices for garnish

In a highball glass filled with ice cubes, stir together the rum and the Rose's lime juice. Fill the glass with tonic water and garnish with lime. Makes 1 cocktail.

SPICED FRUIT PUNCH

10 whole cloves
2 medium oranges, cut into slices
1 lemon, cut into slices
1 46-ounce can pineapple juice
1 32-ounce can apple juice
juice of 1 lemon

3 cinnamon sticks
¼ cup honey
¼ teaspoon allspice
¼ teaspoon ground nutmeg
 (optional)
1 liter ginger ale

Insert cloves into fruit slices. Combine fruit slices and next 8 ingredients in a large stock pot; simmer uncovered for 30 minutes. Remove stick cinnamon. Add ginger ale; heat and serve hot, or let cool, add ice and serve cold. Yield 3 quarts.

DIVINE HOT CHOCOLATE

2½ squares unsweetened
   chocolate, cut into pieces
½ cup water
¾ cup sugar

⅛ teaspoon salt
½ cup cream, whipped
6 cups hot milk, sweetened with 4
   tablespoons sugar

Combine chocolate and water in saucepan and cook over low heat until smooth, stirring constantly. Add sugar and salt and cook stirring constantly until thick; about 5 minutes. Cool. Whip cream until thick. Fold chocolate mixture into cream. Put 2 heaping tablespoons of mixture into mugs. Fill with hot milk; about 8 ounces. Use peppermint or cinnamon stick for stirrer. Serves 6.

WATERMELON PUNCH

1 large watermelon
1 cup sugar
1 cup water

1 33-ounce bottle raspberry ginger
   ale, chilled
1 cup rum (optional)

Cut watermelon in desired shape. (Watermelon shell may be used as punch bowl.) Scoop pulp from melon, remove seeds and mash. Measure 1 gallon juice and set aside. Make sugar syrup from water and sugar. Bring to a boil, reduce heat and simmer 5 minutes. Add to watermelon juice and chill. Just before serving, add ginger ale and rum. Yield 6 quarts.

PINEAPPLE SHERBET PUNCH

Mix together:
5 6-ounce frozen limeades
5 6-ounce frozen lemonades
5 16-ounce frozen orange juice

5 46-ounce cans pineapple juice
6 quarts water
2 teaspoons salt

Refrigerate. When ready to serve, add:

4 quarts ginger ale, chilled

1 pineapple sherbet to each bowl

Yield 5 gallons.

MIMOSA PUNCH

5 large oranges
15 maraschino cherries
rose leaves, washed and dried
⅓ cup sugar
3 2½-inch cinnamon sticks

3 cups orange juice
¼ cup orange flavored liqueur
¼ cup brandy
1 1-liter bottle club soda, chilled
1 750-ml champagne

Ice Ring: Prepare day ahead. Cut a continuous 1 inch wide strip of peel from each orange; reserve. Squeeze juices from oranges; add water to orange juice to measure 5 cups liquid. Pour 3½ cups mixture into 6 cup ring mold; freeze until frozen, about 3 hours. Refrigerate remaining mixture. Roll orange peel strips into roses, secure with toothpick. When ring is frozen, arrange orange peel roses and rose leaves, and cherries on frozen mixture; pour in half of remaining juice mixture; freeze until firm enough to set garnishes; about 1 hour. Add remaining juice mixture. Freeze until hard set.

In 1 quart saucepan over high heat, heat sugar, cinnamon sticks and ½ cup water to boiling. Reduce heat to low; cover and simmer 15 minutes. Refrigerate until ready to complete punch.

Just before serving: Use a 6 quart punch bowl. Mix orange juice, liqueur, brandy and cinnamon mixture. Stir in soda and champagne. Unmold ice ring; add to punch. Yield 12 cups or 24 servings.

CAFE BRULOT

2¼ cups Cognac or brandy
½ cup orange peel julienne
36 whole cloves
32 sugar cubes

12 cinnamon sticks
12 cups freshly brewed strong
    coffee

Heat Cognac with orange peel, cloves, sugar and cinnamon in heavy large saucepan. Tilt pan and ignite. When flames subside, stir until sugar dissolves. Add coffee and heat through. Ladle into cups. Yield 12 servings.

CRANBERRY LIQUEUR

A special holiday treat!

8 cups cranberries, picked over   **4 cups gin**
4 cups sugar

In food processor chip cranberries in batches. Divide between 2 sterilized 2 quart glass jars with nonmetallic lids. Divide the sugar and the gin between the jars and seal the jars. Shake mixture vigorously for 5 seconds to blend well. Store in cool place, shaking it once a day, for 3 weeks. Strain mixture through a fine sieve into a bowl, pressing lightly on cranberries to extract the liquid. Transfer to decanter. Makes about 6 cups.

YELLOW PUNCH

This recipe is great for a 50th wedding anniversary celebration. It was shared with us by our friend E. E. Tynes. Tynes also keeps us supplied with tapes of beautiful piano music we use at the restaurant.

3 small packages orange jello   **3 small cans frozen lemon juice**
3 small packages lemon jello   **1 ounce almond extract**
3 tall cans pineapple juice   **8 cups sugar**
3 small cans frozen orange juice

Dissolve sugar in 3 pints hot water. Add jello to sugar and water while hot. Stir to dissolve well and cool. When cooled down, add juices and almond extract. Chill till ready to serve. Add enough cold water to make 5 gallons of punch.

DIXIE TEA

Dip rims of 2 cups in water and coat with sugar. Add:

2 cups hot tea

Into each cup of tea add:
1 ounce Amaretto   **½ ounce Grand Marnier**

Stir and serve immediately. Serves 2.

CRAB MOLD

1 teaspoon unflavored gelatin	1 2-ounce jar pimentos, sliced,
¼ cup water	chopped, and drained
2 8-ounce packages cream cheese	8 ounces crab meat
2 tablespoons sherry	⅛ teaspoon ground black pepper
¾ teaspoon seasoned salt	¼ cup snipped parsley
	1 tablespoon lemon juice

Sprinkle gelatin over water to soften; cook over low heat until dissolved; beat into cream cheese until smooth. Add all other ingredients and stir until mixed well. Pour into desired formed mold or bowl, and refrigerate several hours, or until set. Turn out onto plate covered with leaf lettuce, and garnish with tomato rose.

Line inside of bowl or mold with plastic wrap before adding mixture for easiest removal.

Serve with crackers, toasted baguettes, or sliced cucumbers.

STUFFED ARTICHOKE BOTTOMS

8 to 10 artichoke bottoms
¼ cup Monterey Jack cheese
6 strips bacon
8 ounces white lump crab meat
2 tablespoons green bell pepper,
    finely diced
1 tablespoon onion, finely diced

1 large clove garlic, minced
½ teaspoon salt
½ teaspoon pepper
1 cup bread crumbs
½ teaspoon dried basil
½ stick butter
2 tablespoons lemon juice

Fry bacon until crisp. Drain and crumble. Lightly brown artichoke bottoms in bacon drippings. Remove from skillet and drain. Sauté bell pepper, onion and garlic in remaining bacon drippings until tender. Remove from skillet, drain and cool. Combine crab meat, bell pepper mixture, bacon, cheese and 2 tablespoons melted butter. Scoop small amount from center of artichoke bottom and mound mixture into each. Mix bread crumbs, basil, butter and lemon juice. Firmly pat crumb mixture on top of artichokes. Bake in pre-heated 350 degree oven for 12 to 15 minutes until golden brown. Serve immediately.

STUFFED MUSHROOMS

24 whole jumbo mushrooms
1½ cups shredded Monterey Jack
    cheese
2 teaspoons garlic, minced
1 cup freshly processed bread
    crumbs

4 tablespoons melted butter
⅓ cup red wine
½ teaspoon salt
½ teaspoon pepper

Brush mushrooms and remove stems. Blend all remaining ingredients well. Do not process. Brush tops of mushrooms with additional melted butter. Stuff each mushroom with mixture being careful not to mound as mixture will cook over during baking. Bake on greased baking sheet at 350 degrees for 10 to 15 minutes until cheese in mixture has melted. Do not bake until mushrooms have become soft. Serves 8 to 12 depending on size of mushrooms. Leftover stuffing freezes well.

MUSHROOM TURNOVERS

1 8-ounce package cream cheese,
    softened
1½ cups plain flour
1 stick butter, softened
½ pound mushrooms, diced
1 medium onion, diced

¼ cup sour cream
1 teaspoon salt
½ teaspoon white pepper
1 teaspoon minced garlic
2 eggs, beaten

Beat cream cheese, flour and butter until smooth. Shape into ball, wrap and refrigerate for about one hour until chilled. Sauté mushrooms, onion and garlic in two tablespoons olive oil until tender. Stir in sour cream, salt, pepper and two tablespoons plain flour and set aside. On well floured surface using a floured rolling pin, roll out half of dough ⅛ inch thick. Cut out dough with three inch round cookie cutter. Repeat with remaining dough. Put about 1½ teaspoons mushroom mixture onto one half of pastry round. Moisten edges of pastry with beaten egg. Fold pastry over filling and press edges together with floured tines of fork. Prick top of turnover once with fork to allow steam to escape. Put turnovers on ungreased cookie sheet and brush lightly with remaining egg mixture. Bake in preheated 450 degree oven ten to twelve minutes or until golden brown. Makes about three dozen turnovers.

MARINATED BABY CARROTS

2 pounds baby carrots
1 medium green pepper
1 medium red pepper
1 small onion
1 can condensed tomato soup
½ cup lite vegetable oil

1 cup sugar
1 teaspoon prepared mustard
1 teaspoon Worcestershire sauce
salt
pepper

Cook carrots in salted water until medium done. Rinse in cold water. Arrange layers of carrots, pepper strips and onion rings in a bowl. Combine remaining ingredients in a saucepan and bring to a boil, stirring occasionally until sugar has dissolved. Pour marinade over vegetables and refrigerate overnight. Serves 12.

DEEP FRIED PICKLED OKRA

We also use pickled okra as a garnish in our Bloody Marys.

1 pound jar of pickled okra,
    drained
2 eggs
1 teaspoon homemade hot pepper
    sauce or Tabasco

½ cup flour
½ cup white cornmeal
dash salt

Beat together eggs, milk, pepper sauce and salt. Roll okra in flour. Dip in egg mixture. Dredge in cornmeal. Fry in deep oil until brown. Serves 12.

TURNIP GREEN DIP
AND JALAPEÑO MUFFINS

1 10-ounce package frozen turnip
    or collard greens, thawed and
    well drained
¼ teaspoon grated lemon rind
½ cup finely chopped onion
2 tablespoons butter, melted
½ pound sliced mushrooms
1 teaspoon chopped garlic

1 8-ounce package herbed cream
    cheese (Boursin or make your
    own)
1 8-ounce package regular cream
    cheese
1 teaspoon Worcestershire sauce
Tabasco, to taste
Jalapeño Muffins (see below)

Process turnip greens and lemon rind till finely chopped. Cook onion, garlic and mushrooms in butter until tender. Do not burn. Stir in turnip mixture, cream cheeses, Worcestershire sauce and hot sauce. Cook till blended and heated through. Serve in chafing dish with muffins. Serves 25.

JALAPEÑO MUFFINS

2 cups jalapeño cornbread mix
1 large egg, beaten

1 cup buttermilk
2 tablespoons oil

Mix all together and bake in prepared mini-muffin pans. Bake at 400 degrees for 11 minutes. Yield approximately 50 muffins.

MINI CRÊPES WITH ASPARAGUS

Crêpe Batter
fresh asparagus spears, steamed

1 5-ounce package Boursin or
    Rondele cheese (room
    temperature)

Make crêpes about 3 inches in diameter. Stack between sheets of wax paper.
Place steamed asparagus (trimmed to about 4 inches) spears on crêpe spread
with cheese. Asparagus tip should extend about ½ inch out of crêpe. Roll
spear in crêpe. Serve at room temperature.

Crêpe Batter:
1 cup all purpose flour
dash salt
¾ cup water

4 eggs
¾ to 1 cup milk
2 tablespoons butter, melted

Blend in blender. Stop machine once and scrape down sides. Chill one hour.
Heat a crêpe pan. Grease lightly. Ladle about 3 tablespoons batter on pan.
Tilt in all directions so batter covers bottom. Cook about 1 minute or until
lightly browned. Quickly turn and cook on other side about 15 seconds. Place
wax paper or deli sheets between crêpes. May be frozen.

BLACK-EYED PEA FRITTERS

Combine and mix well:
2 cups plain flour
2 teaspoons baking powder

1 teaspoon salt
4 eggs

Add to flour mixture:
3 cups black-eyed peas, drained
    and rinsed
⅔ cup diced green bell peppers
½ cup diced onion

1 tablespoon sugar
1 teaspoon minced garlic
1 tomato, seeded and chopped

Drop by teaspoonfuls into deep oil (350 degrees) for 4 to 5 minutes, or until
golden brown. Remove with slotted spoon and drain on paper towels. Serve
hot with your favorite dipping sauce. Serves 20 (2 fritters each).

SQUASH TARTLETS

2 recipes cream cheese pastry
2 pounds yellow crookneck squash
½ large onion, chopped
2 tablespoons fresh herbs (thyme, parsley, basil or chives)
½ pound softened cream cheese
3 eggs
½ cup heavy cream
½ teaspoon grated fresh nutmeg (optional)
½ pound Cheddar cheese, grated (about 2 cups)
salt and pepper, to taste

Filling: Wash, slice and cook squash and onion, salt and pepper in just enough water to cover until tender. Drain, mashing down to extract as much liquid as possible. Process with cream cheese, eggs, herbs. Add heavy cream and cheese. Fill tart shells with mixture. Bake at 375 degrees until puffy; about 10 minutes. Serve warm. Yield about 60 tartlets.

Pastry:
2 cups plain flour
2 sticks butter, softened
1 8-ounce package cream cheese, softened

Beat together and chill for 30 minutes. Press into mini-muffin tins.

COUNTRY CAVIAR

24 ounces drained blackeyed peas, (canned)
¼ cup chopped bell pepper
¼ cup chopped red pepper
¼ cup minced jalapeño pepper
½ cup diced onion
¼ cup drained chopped pimentos
½ cup sliced water chestnuts
2 tablespoons garlic, minced

Toss above ingredients together and marinate with:
¼ cup red wine vinegar
½ cup olive oil
1 tablespoon Dijon mustard
salt and Tabasco to taste

Marinate overnight. Mash mixture slightly to thicken and serve with tortilla chips.

VEGETABLE PLATTER EXTRAVAGANZA

Rose Hill likes this better than the ordinary veggie tray.
Your guests will love it.

2 heads cauliflowerets
1 pound baby carrots, cut in half
   lengthwise
1 pound celery sticks
1 pound button mushrooms
2 cups yellow squash, sliced ¼
   inch thick

1 pint cherry tomatoes
1½ cups Monterey jack cheese,
   cubed
2 cups large green olives
1 pound pepperoni, sliced ⅛ inch
   thick
2 cups Greek peppers

Marinade:
1½ cups vegetable oil
3 cups tarragon vinegar
½ cup sugar
4 cloves garlic, minced

1 tablespoon prepared mustard
1 tablespoon salt
2 teaspoons tarragon leaves
1 teaspoon black pepper

Combine all ingredients. Mix with electric mixer until sugar dissolves. Pour over cauliflower, carrots, celery, olives, peppers and mushrooms. Chill 8 hours, tossing occasionally. Several hours before serving, add squash, cherry tomatoes, cheese and pepperoni. Remove from bowl with slotted spoon. Place on platter lined with leaf lettuce. Very colorful and good.

CURRIED PECAN CHEESE BALL

4 cups grated Cheddar cheese
8 ounce cream cheese, softened
½ cup chutney, processed
½ cup mayonnaise

1 cup toasted pecans, finely
   chopped
1 tablespoon curry powder

Beat cheeses and mayonnaise until smooth. Add remaining ingredients and mix well. Shape into ball and cover with plastic wrap. Refrigerate overnight. Let stand at room temperature for 30 minutes before serving. Wonderful served with Swedish gingersnaps or your favorite cracker.

SUN DRIED TOMATO
AND CHIVE CHEESE BALL

16 ounces cream cheese, softened
¼ cup sun dried tomatoes, diced
½ cup chives, chopped

½ cup bacon, fried crisp and
   chopped
2 tablespoons mayonnaise

Soak tomatoes 1 hour. Drain and pat dry. Beat cream cheese and mayonnaise until smooth. Gently work remaining ingredients in with hands. Shape into ball or desired shape and refrigerate for several hours. Let stand at room temperature for 30 minutes before serving.

TORTELLINI WITH
PARSLEY-CAPER SAUCE

½ pound small fresh or frozen
   cheese tortellini
½ cup olive oil
1 ounce Parmesan cheese
1 clove garlic
2 tablespoons sunflower seeds

2 tablespoons capers
¾ cup tightly packed flat-leaf
   parsley
salt and pepper to taste
dash of fresh lemon juice

Cook tortellini in large pot of boiling, salted water until just done (about 8 minutes). Drain; rinse with cold water.

For the sauce, grate the cheese. Drop garlic clove into food processor, whir 10 seconds. Add parsley, lemon juice, salt and pepper until just blended. Add olive oil slowly just until emulsified. Stir in capers and sunflower seeds. Pour over tortellini and cool. Serve speared on skewers.

CORN CAKES WITH CAVIAR

1½ cups corn kernels, fresh
    (3 ears) or frozen
1⅓ cups milk
1 tablespoon white self-rising
    cornmeal
1 tablespoon sugar

¼ teaspoon salt
2 eggs
3 tablespoons cake flour
1 cup sour cream
¼ cup oil
Caviar Topping

Cut corn kernels from the cobs. Cook kernels with the milk over medium heat until milk is evaporated and corn is tender. Process in food processor until smooth. Cool. Recipe may be made to this point 1 day ahead.

Assembly: In a processor, combine corn purée, cornmeal, sugar, salt, eggs, cake flour and sour cream. Blend until thoroughly mixed. Let rest 15 to 20 minutes. Drop batter by tablespoons into pan brushed with oil over medium heat, turning once, until browned, about 1 minute per side.

Topping:
2 ounces salmon caviar
2 ounces golden caviar

¼ cup sour cream
⅛ teaspoon lemon juice

Drain the caviar. In a bowl, gently fold caviars and lemon juice into sour cream. Put dollop of topping on each corn cake. Yield 30 hors d'oeuvres.

CURRIED CHICKEN DEVILED EGGS

2 3-ounce packages cream cheese,
    softened
⅔ cup plain yogurt (room
    temperature)
1 tablespoon + 1 teaspoon curry
    powder
1 tablespoon lemon juice

¼ teaspoon salt
⅛ teaspoon pepper
2 cups finely chopped cooked
    chicken
¾ cup raisins
1 dozen boiled eggs, peeled, halved
    and yolks removed

Beat cream cheese in large mixing bowl on medium speed until smooth. Add yogurt, curry powder, lemon juice, salt and pepper; mix well. Stir in remaining ingredients. Mash about 6 cooked egg yolks up and blend in. Mayonnaise may be added if too stiff. Use pastry tube or spoon to fill egg halves. Sprinkle paprika on tops before serving. Yield 24 halves.

BEEF TENDERLOIN ON YEAST ROLLS

4 pounds beef tenderloin, side
    muscle and fat removed, silver
    peeled
2 tablespoons olive oil

2 teaspoons salt
1 teaspoon coarse ground pepper
2 tablespoons soy sauce

Mix olive oil and soy sauce together. Brush tenderloin with mixture and rub with salt and pepper. Bake for 45 minutes in preheated 350 degree oven. Meat should be medium depending on weight and oven variations. Allow to cool completely. Slice ⅛ inch thick and lay in tenderloin juices until ready to stuff rolls. Stuff in yeast rolls or angel biscuits (see index) 30 minutes before serving. Stuffing too early will cause bread to become soggy. Warm in low oven or serve room temperature. Serve with Horseradish Sauce or Curried Mayonnaise. Tenderloin will stuff 60 to 75 party size rolls. Allow 2 to 3 per person because guests, especially the men, eat them like popcorn.

CURRIED MAYONNAISE

1 cup mayonnaise
1 teaspoon lemon juice

2 teaspoons curry powder
1 teaspoon sugar

Combine all ingredients, and refrigerate overnight, or for at least 3 to 4 hours.

HORSERADISH SAUCE

1 cup sour cream
½ cup mayonnaise
1 tablespoon horseradish (or more,
    to taste)

½ teaspoon salt
½ teaspoon pepper
1 tablespoon chopped fresh parsley

Combine all ingredients, and refrigerate overnight, or for at least 3 to 4 hours.

HERBED FRENCH BREAD AND TENDERLOIN

1 4-pound beef tenderloin
olive oil
salt

pepper, coarsely ground
2 loaves French bread

Remove fat, side muscle, and peel silver from tenderloin. Rub generously with olive oil, salt and pepper. Bake in 350 degree oven for 1 hour. Let cool completely. Slice as thin as possible without shredding. You should have approximately eighty slices.

Slice French bread into ½ inch slices. (You'll get about 50 slices from one loaf.) Spread each slice of bread with herbed butter and top each with a slice of tenderloin. Top each with small dollop of horseradish sauce. Serves 30 to 40.

Herbed Butter:
1 pound butter (room temperature)
2 teaspoons minced garlic

2 teaspoons fresh basil, chopped
1 teaspoon Krazy Jane salt

Cream together well. Let sit for several hours and beat again.

Horseradish Sauce:
½ pint sour cream
1 tablespoon horseradish

1 teaspoon black pepper
½ teaspoon salt

Mix together well. Let chill in refrigerator for several hours.
Note: Your butcher will remove side muscle and silver for you.

HICKORY SMOKED TURKEY SPREAD

2 cups hickory smoked turkey,
  chopped fine (about 1 pound)
1 cup pecans, chopped fine
½ cup mayonnaise

¼ cup celery, chopped fine
garlic, to taste
¼ cup sweet pickle relish, drained
  (optional)

Mix all ingredients together. Spread on crackers or toast points.

ROSE HILL MEAT BALLS

Meatballs:

2 pounds ground round
1 cup corn flake crumbs
⅓ cup parsley flakes
2 eggs
2 tablespoons soy sauce

¼ teaspoon pepper
½ teaspoon garlic powder
⅓ cup ketchup
2 tablespoons finely minced onion

Mix and form into small balls. Arrange in baking pan. Pour sauce over and bake 30 minutes in 350 degree oven.

Sauce:

1 1-pound can jellied cranberry
   sauce
1 12-ounce bottle chili sauce

2 tablespoons brown sugar
1 tablespoon bottled lemon juice
¼ cup bourbon

Combine and cook in medium saucepan over medium heat, stirring constantly until smooth. Yield 130 melon ball size or 60 large.

SAUSAGE PINWHEELS

½ cup shortening
2 cups plain flour
1 teaspoon salt

2 pounds lean ground sausage,
   mild or hot

Cut shortening into dry ingredients. Add enough milk to make a stiff dough. Divide dough into two pieces and roll out into square. Spread each square with 1 pound sausage within ¼ inch of edges. Moisten edges with water and roll up in jelly roll fashion. Freeze. Remove 20 minutes before slicing. Slice ¼ inch and bake on cookie sheet in preheated 400 degree oven for 15 to 20 minutes. Drain on paper towels. Puff paste found in some grocery stores may be substituted for dough.

BAKED HAM WITH ANGEL BISCUITS

Bake a whole, fully cooked ham. We prefer a Hamilton Easy Karv ham, but we only bake it for 8 minutes per pound, as the suggested cooking time on the label may cause the ham to become too dry during baking. There is no danger of undercooking the ham, since it is already fully cooked.

Prepare the Old Fashioned Buttermilk biscuit recipe (see index). Roll out dough to ½ inch thickness. Cut out with 2 inch biscuit cutter, and place on greased pan. Brush with butter and bake at 450 degrees for 10 to 15 minutes, until tops are golden brown. Biscuits will double in thickness when cooked. When cut with a 2 inch cutter, dough will make 2½ to 3 dozen biscuits. Scraps from dough can be gingerly pressed together, and cut to make more biscuits. When done, place the biscuits in a linen lined basket, and the ham on a large platter. Garnish ham with large bunches of flat leaf (Italian) parsley or mounds of fresh fruit. Serve with chutney, mayonnaise and honey mustard. This will be irresistible to your guests.

CORNBREAD WITH HONEY BAKED HAM AND SORGHUM BUTTER

1 recipe Rose Hill cornbread
    (see pg. 107)
8 thin slices honey baked ham
1 stick softened butter
1 tablespoon pure sorghum syrup

¼ teaspoon Dijon mustard
¼ cup chopped parsley
¼ cup coarsely ground black
    pepper

Make cornbread. Pour into 12 x 8 inch baking pan sprayed with vegetable oil. Bake in preheated 425 degree oven 10 to 15 minutes until cornbread is brown. Allow to cool in pan. When cool, turn cornbread onto a baking sheet. With a long serrated knife, trim to ⅜-inch thickness.

Combine softened butter with syrup and mustard; spread on cornbread. Cover with ham slices and refrigerate until butter is firm. Cut out canapés, using your favorite shaped cutter, or cut into bite sized pieces with a serrated knife. Garnish with parsley and black pepper.

ONION MARMALADE WITH HAM BISCUITS

In skillet combine:

1 tablespoon olive oil and 3
   tablespoons butter

2 cups sliced sweet onions
   (preferably Vidalia)
⅛ teaspoon red pepper flakes

Cook uncovered about 5 minutes.

Add:

⅓ cup chopped pitted prunes
¼ cup Sweet Marsala
3 tablespoons brown sugar
2 tablespoons cider vinegar

1 teaspoon freshly grated ginger
   root
¼ teaspoon salt

Reduce heat to low and cook uncovered 12 to 15 minutes or until prunes soften and mixture turns dark brown. Cool and refrigerate if not using immediately.

Stuff biscuits with smoked Virginia ham and 1 teaspoon onion marmalade. Wrap in foil and heat in 350 degree oven before serving. May be made a day ahead and stored in airtight container. Yummy! See index for biscuit recipe.

PRAWNS IN GINGER SAUCE

1 tablespoon olive oil
3 teaspoons fresh grated ginger
   root
12 uncooked large prawns or
   jumbo shrimp, shelled and
   deveined

1 tablespoon garlic, minced
3 teaspoons sesame oil
⅓ cup light soy sauce
¼ cup white wine
1 tablespoon rice wine vinegar
2 tablespoons honey

Heat olive oil in skillet until medium hot but not smoking. Add ginger and stir for about one minute. Add prawns and sauté just until pink on both sides, about 3 minutes. Do not overcook! Combine soy sauce, garlic, sesame oil , wine, vinegar and honey. Mix well, pour over prawns and toss gently. Cover and refrigerate overnight. Bring prawns to room temperature before serving. Serves 4 to 6. Also good served warm over rice as an entrée.

CATFISH NUGGETS

Prepare catfish croquet mixture. (See index).

Form mixture into 1 inch balls, roll in cornmeal, and deep fry until golden brown.

These will hold well in a warm oven, and make a great presentation mounded in a basket lined with a country print napkin. Serve with your favorite cocktail sauce or tartar sauce (see below). Makes approximately 50.

TARTAR SAUCE

2 cups real mayonnaise
2 tablespoons fresh lemon juice
1 small onion, grated

½ cup dill pickle relish
1 teaspoon Krazy Jane salt
½ teaspoon black pepper

Mix all ingredients. Let chill for several hours.

GOAT CHEESE WITH
SUN DRIED TOMATO SALSA

6 dried tomato halves
3 cloves garlic, pressed
2 tablespoons olive oil
1 tablespoon chopped fresh
   rosemary

1 tablespoon chopped fresh basil
1 French baguette
olive oil
1 10-ounce package goat cheese

Cover dried tomatoes with boiling water and let stand 5 minutes; drain and chop. Combine tomatoes and next 4 ingredients. Set aside.

Slice baguette into ¼ inch slices, brush with olive oil and toast in 350 degree oven until light brown (do not over-toast). Place whole goat cheese on serving platter. Spoon salsa over. Garnish with fresh rosemary sprigs. Place baguette slices around cheese for spreading. Serves 8.

CHEESE STRAWS

1 pound sharp Cheddar cheese	2 cups flour
¼ pound softened margarine	½ teaspoon cayenne pepper

Let cheese come to room temperature. Mix cheese and margarine together by hand. Mix in flour and pepper, also by hand. It is important not to use an electric mixer in order to prevent overworking the dough. Form the dough into a large roll and insert into a cookie press. Using a star tip, press onto a cookie sheet in long strips. Bake at 350 degrees for 12 to 15 minutes. After first 5 minutes turn the pan 180 degrees. Turn again after 5 more minutes, to promote even cooking and prevent burning. Check again after 2 more minutes, to avoid over cooking. Cool and break into 2 to 3 inch pieces. Layer between paper towels overnight. Keep in an airtight container.

CHEESE AND DATE WAFERS

½ pound New York Sharp	1 teaspoon baking powder
Cheddar Cheese, grated	1 teaspoon salt
1 stick butter	¼ teaspoon cayenne pepper
1½ cups plain flour	pitted dates

Cream cheese and butter. Sift dry ingredients together and add to cheese mixture. Mix well but do not over beat. Pinch off pieces of dough about quarter size. Mash out and place ¼ slice of date in center and pinch top together. Bake in preheated 375 degree oven until just golden. About 10 minutes.

QUICK PÂTÉ

8 ounces liver sausage
8 ounces cream cheese
1 cup sliced mushrooms

¼ cup champagne
freshly ground pepper to taste

Sauté mushrooms in 1 tablespoon butter. Process all ingredients in processor and chill for several hours.

BLACK-EYED PEA PÂTÉ

4 cups black-eyed peas, canned
4 fresh tomatoes, finely chopped
3 chopped green onions
2 jalapeño peppers, grated or finely chopped

¼ cup ketchup
6 dashes Tabasco sauce
2 envelopes unflavored gelatin
⅓ cup mayonnaise

Drain peas and add gelatin to juice and heat until gelatin is dissolved. Process ½ of the peas and add gelatin mixture, remaining peas and all other ingredients. Add salt to taste and stir well. Chill overnight in mold. To serve, unmold on crisp bed of leaf lettuce and garnish. Serve with favorite cracker or our favorite is fried cornbread in 2 inch rounds. See index for Spoon Bread.

GARBAGE DIP

*This wonderful recipe was shared with us by
our friend Gloria Walker, one of the BEST cooks in Montgomery.*

1 cup pitted chopped ripe olives
3 to 4 chopped green onions (tops, too)
3 to 4 chopped and seeded ripe tomatoes

1 small can drained green chilies
1 tablespoon olive oil
dash Tabasco
dash garlic salt
½ tablespoon wine vinegar

Mix all ingredients. Let marinate at least 24 hours. Serve with king-sized Fritos.

CRAB MEAT DIP

1 clove garlic, cut in half
⅓ cup heavy cream
1 8-ounce package cream cheese,
    softened
1½ teaspoons Worcestershire
    sauce

dash Tabasco sauce
1 cup flaked crab meat
2 teaspoons lemon juice
dash salt
dash pepper

Rub a bowl with garlic clove. Gradually add the cream to softened cream cheese in the bowl rubbed with garlic. Blend until smooth. Add remaining ingredients and mix well. Serve with crackers, chips or toast points that have been brushed with olive oil before toasting.

MA'S SHRIMP DIP

This is Barbara's sons', Bill, Jr., Brad & Bart McCorvey's favorite seafood dip.
It is a Christmas buffet tradition.

1 8-ounce package cream cheese,
    softened
6 ounces canned shrimp, rinsed
    and drained, or freshly cooked
    shrimp, diced

3 tablespoons chili sauce
2 teaspoons Worcestershire sauce
2 teaspoons grated onion
juice of 1 large lemon
½ cup mayonnaise

Combine all ingredients. Let chill 24 hours before serving. Serve with large corn chips.

PERFECT POTATO CHIPS

4 baking potatoes (1½ pounds), sliced thin

3 quarts vegetable oil
coarse or seasoned salt

Peel potatoes and slice paper thin with a vegetable peeler or a mandoline. Soak slices in 3 quarts cold water for 1 hour, changing water every 20 minutes. Drain and dry potato slices on paper towels. Heat oil in Dutch oven to 350 degrees (no hotter). Working in batches, fry potato slices until golden brown (about 1 minute). Drain potato chips on paper towels, sprinkle with salt to taste, and serve.

GLAZED PECANS

¼ cup sour cream
½ cup brown sugar
¼ cup white sugar

1 teaspoon vanilla
1½ cups whole pecans

Bring sour cream and sugars to a boil. Add vanilla and pecans, and pour mixture out onto a lightly greased baking sheet to cool, separating pecans with a fork. Store in an airtight container.

WHITE TRASH

We don't know where this title came from, but we get a kick out of telling people the name of this recipe. We especially loved it when the ladies of a local Episcopal church served it at their bridge club.

1 12-ounce box Golden Graham cereal
1 12-ounce box raisins
3 cups roasted peanuts
2 cups peanut butter

1 12-ounce package chocolate chips
1 stick oleo
1 16-ounce box confectioner's sugar

Mix cereal, raisins and peanuts in large container. Melt oleo, peanut butter and chocolate chips, stirring until blended. Let cool. Pour over dry mixture and mix well. (Hands may be necessary at this point.) Layer ½ powdered sugar, cereal mixture, and remaining powdered sugar in large paper or plastic bag. Shake to coat. Keeps well in airtight container.

Most couples say "I DO" right on our front porch.

$\mathcal{S}$oups
and
$\mathcal{S}$tews

The happy couple cut another beautiful wedding cake.

Another wedding on the porch of Rose Hill.

COLD PEACH SOUP

1½ pounds peaches, peeled, pitted
    and sliced
2 cups sour cream
sugar, to taste (depends on
    tartness of peaches)

1 cup fresh orange juice
1 cup pineapple juice
½ cup peach schnapps
1 tablespoon fresh lemon juice

Purée peaches in processor. Add remaining ingredients. Strain. Serve chilled in melon bowls. Yield 8 servings.
Cantaloupe may be added to this.

COLD MELON SOUP

A favorite at ladies' luncheons.

2 cups cubed cantaloupe
2 cups cubed honeydew
1 cup sliced strawberries
1½ cups orange juice

⅓ cup fresh lime juice
4 tablespoons honey
1 to 1½ cups sparkling white
    wine, chilled

Purée all ingredients except wine and chill overnight. Add chilled wine just before serving. If desired, add additional honey for sweeter soup. Serve with Swedish gingersnaps. Serves 6.

ZUCCHINI & CREAM CHEESE SOUP

6 cups sliced zucchini
1 large onion, diced
8 ounces cream cheese, softened
2 cups chicken broth

1 teaspoon salt
1 teaspoon fresh ground pepper
½ to 1 teaspoon fresh dill weed

Cook zucchini, onion, chicken broth, dill, salt and pepper until zucchini is tender. Process zucchini and stock gradually adding pinches of the cream cheese. Heat before serving, do not boil! Garnish with fresh sprig of dill. Serves 6 to 8.

CUCUMBER EGG PETAL SOUP

This recipe was developed by Dr. Haywood Bartlett, Mrs. Edgar's employer for 23 years. They loved to develop recipes together.

1 teaspoon cooking oil
1 scallion, chopped
½ cup thinly sliced unpeeled
    cucumber
1 teaspoon salt
4 cups stock or chicken broth
1 teaspoon soy sauce

dash pepper
¼ teaspoon monosodium
    glutamate (optional)
2 tablespoons cornstarch
2 tablespoons cold water
1 egg, slightly beaten

Heat oil. Add half of chopped scallion, then cucumber. Give it a few stirs. Add salt and stock. Bring to a boil and simmer 2 minutes. Add soy sauce, pepper and monosodium glutamate. Mix cornstarch with 2 tablespoons cold water into soup. Cook until soup is slightly thickened. Dribble egg mixture into soup while stirring soup around gently. Remove from heat. Wait until egg petals float to surface. DO NOT OVERCOOK unless you want hard boiled eggs in your soup. Serve with remaining scallion sprinkled on top. Yield 4 servings.

CREAM OF SQUASH SOUP

At Rose Hill we call this "Vishysquash".

4 cups sliced yellow squash
1 large onion, diced
½ stick butter
1½ cups chicken broth

1½ cups half & half
1 teaspoon salt
½ teaspoon white pepper

Cook squash, onion, and butter in broth until squash is tender. Purée squash with stock in processor. Add half & half, salt and pepper and heat. Do not boil! Garnish with fresh sprigs of parsley. Serves 6.

VEGETABLE SOUP

Ma always convinced us this would cure a cold.

1 pound ground chuck

Brown ground chuck in large pot. Drain. Add:

3 quarts water
6 chicken bouillon cubes
3 chopped ribs celery
3 peeled and chopped carrots

3 peeled and cubed potatoes
1 large onion, peeled and diced
2 cups sliced okra

1 can tomatoes
1 can tomato juice

1 can French style green beans,
    drained
1 can English peas, drained

Purée tomatoes and tomato juice. Add to soup. Add beans and peas. Cook on low heat until vegetables are tender. It may be necessary to add water if mixture becomes too thick.

DABBO'S CHICKEN AND DUMPLINGS

2¼ pounds pulled chicken, dark
  and white
4 cups chicken broth

3 tablespoons butter
salt and pepper to taste

Canned chicken broth may be added if there's not enough broth after cooking chicken.

DUMPLINGS

1 cup plain flour
1½ teaspoons baking powder
½ teaspoon salt

2 tablespoons vegetable oil
½ cup milk

Sift dry ingredients together. Add oil and milk. Knead dough gently incorporating additional ½ cup plain flour to form a soft ball. Roll out on floured surface to ⅛ inch thick and cut into 1½ inch strips. Drop dumplings into boiling chicken and broth mixture as quickly as possible. Do not stir! Cover, reduce heat and simmer for 15 minutes. Do not lift lid during cooking! Serve immediately. Serves 8.

MA'S DUMPLINGS

¼ cup Crisco
2 cups plain flour
1 teaspoon salt

1 egg
ice water

Cut Crisco into 2 cups plain flour and add 1 teaspoon salt. Add 1 egg. Add enough ice water to make a very stiff dough. Roll out very thin on a floured surface and cut into strips. Drop into chicken broth which has been brought to a rolling boil. Cook until tender.

STEWED CORN

This is a quick way to get the taste of fresh fried corn.

1 package frozen whole kernel
   corn, divided in half
½ cup water

1 heaping tablespoon cornstarch
½ stick butter
salt and pepper to taste

Process ½ package corn with water. Add to remaining corn. Place in skillet with cornstarch, butter, and salt and pepper to taste. Cook on low heat 20 to 30 minutes until thick. Add water as needed.

SHIRLEY'S BRUNSWICK STEW

3 pounds pork roast
3 pounds beef roast
2 pounds cooked, pulled chicken,
   about 2 large fryers
4 pounds fresh tomatoes, peeled
   and diced
1 pound chopped onion
2 pounds potatoes, cooked and
   smashed

3 pounds frozen or fresh white
   corn
32 ounces ketchup
¼ cup Worcestershire sauce
1 teaspoon red pepper flakes
2 tablespoons salt
1 can of your favorite beer
Tabasco sauce to taste

Boil beef and pork until tender. Boil chickens until meat falls off bones. Reserve broth from meats. Remove fat, skin and bones from meats and shred. Cook tomatoes and onions in chicken broth for 30 minutes. Add remaining ingredients, except pork and beef broths. Add enough of the remaining broth to cover and cook slowly for 2 to 3 hours, stirring often. Taste and adjust spices. Canned chicken broth may be added to reach desired consistency. Serves 15 to 20. Freezes well in airtight container.

CHICKEN AND RICE SOUP

8 cups chicken broth
2 cups pulled cooked chicken
1½ cups cooked white rice

1 cup sliced mushrooms
1 cup leeks, sliced
½ stick butter

Sauté mushrooms and leeks until tender over medium heat. Stir all ingredients together in stock pot. Add salt and pepper to taste. Simmer 30 minutes and serve. Serves 10.

ROSE HILL'S CLAM CHOWDER

¼ pound salt pork, chopped
3 cups potatoes, peeled and diced
1 cup green onion, chopped, tops
  only
2 tablespoons minced shallots
1 medium onion, diced
3 large cloves garlic, minced
6 cups fresh tomatoes, peeled,
  seeded and diced

1 quart minced clams
1 tablespoon Worcestershire sauce
2 teaspoons salt
1 teaspoon freshly ground pepper
1 large bay leaf
½ cup freshly snipped parsley
4 cups clam juice

Drain clams, reserving juice. Cook salt pork in a 4 quart stock pot or kettle over low heat until almost crisp. Add potatoes, onions, shallots and garlic and sauté on medium heat for 10 minutes stirring constantly. Add all ingredients, except parsley, and cook gently for 15 to 20 minutes until vegetables are tender. Add bottled clam juice if reserved juice is not enough. If thicker chowder is desired, add 1 cup mashed potatoes. Stir in parsley just before serving. Serves about 8.

SALLY'S CAMP STEW

1 large fryer
1 pork shoulder, 3 to 4 pounds
1 beef roast, 3 to 4 pounds

10 pounds red potatoes
2½ pounds chopped yellow onion
2½ pounds ketchup

Boil or pressure cook meats until tender and cool. Reserve chicken broth. Remove skin, fat and bones. Pull meat. Cook potatoes until tender. Mash water and potatoes with potato masher. Boil onions in reserved chicken broth until tender. Mix together all ingredients in large stock pot and cook over low heat at least 2 hours.

BEEF STEW WITH DROP DUMPLINGS

1 pound sirloin, cut in 1 inch
   cubes
2 cups hot water
½ cup diced carrots
½ cup diced potatoes
¼ cup diced celery
½ cup diced onion

1 clove garlic, minced
½ cup frozen sweet peas
1 bay leaf
1 teaspoon Worcestershire sauce
1 teaspoon salt
½ teaspoon freshly ground pepper
8 ounces tomato sauce

Roll meat in plain flour. Brown in vegetable oil. Spoon out excess oil, leaving no more than 2 tablespoons in pot. Add hot water and simmer for 1 hour. Add carrots, potatoes, celery, onion, garlic, bay leaf, Worcestershire sauce, salt and pepper; continue cooking, covered, for 30 minutes. Add tomato sauce and peas. Bring stew to boiling and drop dumplings from spoon. Do not stir! Cover and simmer without lifting lid for 12 to 15 minutes. Dumplings: Sift 1 cup plain flour, ½ teaspoon salt, and 1½ teaspoon baking powder. Add ½ cup milk and 2 tablespoons vegetable oil. Stir gently.

STEWART'S GUMBO

2 cups chopped onion	1 teaspoon oregano
2 cups chopped celery	2 bay leaves, ground
2 cups chopped green bell pepper	3 tablespoons filé
½ chopped carrot	2 teaspoons Tabasco
1 chopped tomato	1½ sticks margarine
4 cloves garlic	2 8-ounce cans tomato sauce
2 tablespoons red paprika	1 pound okra
1 teaspoon red pepper	salt to taste
2 teaspoons white pepper	1 small chicken
1 teaspoon black pepper	1 pound shrimp
1 teaspoon thyme	turkey sausage

Remove the skin from the chicken. Peel and devein shrimp. Combine the first 16 ingredients with the flour and cook over high heat for five minutes stirring constantly. Reduce heat and add tomato sauce stirring constantly for another five minutes. Add the chicken with eight cups of water and reduce heat to low and cook for one hour, stirring occasionally. Remove the chicken and debone and return the chicken to the pot. Cook for another thirty minutes after adding the okra and sausage and add the shrimp during the last five minutes. Remove from heat and let stand after adding salt to taste and serve over rice.

RECIPE FOR PRESERVING A HUSBAND

When you've made your selection, let it remain ever settled and give your entire thoughts to preparation for domestic use. Some keep them in pickles, others in hot water. Even poor varieties may be made sweet, tender, and good by garnishing with patience, well-sweetened with smiles and flavored with kisses. Wrap in a mantle of charity, keep warm with a steady fire of domestic devotion. Serve often with peaches and cream. When thus prepared, husband will keep for years!

"Bob"
the daddy
of them all.

$\mathcal{S}$alads
and
$\mathcal{C}$ondiments

"Babs"
with two
of her babies.

Easter Sunday.
Bob lets little ones
feed the animals.
Parents love
the break.

BLUEBERRY CONGEALED SALAD

2 small packages blackberry jello
2 cups boiling water
16 ounces canned blueberries, drained
8 ounces fresh pineapple, finely diced
½ cup walnuts, chopped
1 8-ounce package cream cheese
1 teaspoon lemon zest
½ cup sugar
1 cup sour cream
1 teaspoon vanilla flavoring

Dissolve jello in boiling water. Drain blueberries and reserve juice. Add pineapple juice to juice of berries to measure 1 cup. Add to jello and cool. Stir in berries, pineapple and walnuts. Pour into 2 quart dish and refrigerate until congealed. Cream cheese, sour cream, sugar, vanilla and lemon zest until light and creamy. Spread over jello mixture. Good enough to be dessert. Serves 8 to 10.

STRAWBERRY CONGEALED SALAD

2 small packages strawberry jello
1 cup boiling water
2 10-ounce packages sliced frozen strawberries
1 4-ounce can crushed pineapple
3 medium bananas, mashed
1 cup chopped pecans
1 pint sour cream

Combine jello and water; stir until jello is dissolved. Fold in thawed strawberries and juice, drained pineapple, bananas and nuts. Put half of mixture in 12 X 18 inch dish. Refrigerate until firm. Spread on sour cream and then rest of strawberry mixture. Refrigerate until firm. Serves 8 to 10.

FROZEN FRUIT SALAD

½ cup mayonnaise
1 cup whipping cream
2 cups chopped canned fruit

⅓ cup sugar
1 teaspoon lemon juice

Mix mayonnaise and lemon juice with fruit. Add sugar to cream and beat. Fold into fruit mixture. Freeze in cupcake paper cups in muffin pans until firm. Peel off cupcake cups and serve on lettuce leaf topped with dab of mayonnaise.

CRANBERRY SALAD

1 pound raw cranberries
1 orange
2 cups sugar
1 large apple, chopped fine
2 small packages cherry jello

2 cups boiling water
2 cups ice water
1 small can crushed pineapple
   (do not drain)

Grind cranberries and orange. Add chopped apple. Mix jello with boiling water. When dissolved, add ice water. Add crushed pineapple (do not drain) and jello to cranberry mixture. Place in mold and chill until set.

AVOCADO SALAD

2 well ripened avocados, 1 mashed
   and 1 cubed
1 small apple, chopped
1 small can crushed pineapple
⅓ cup chopped pecans

1 package lime jello
½ cup boiling water
½ cup whipping cream
½ cup mayonnaise

Mix lime jello with boiling water, set aside to cool, but not congeal. Combine jello with mayonnaise and mashed avocado. Add all other ingredients except cream. Whip cream until it forms soft peaks. Fold whipped cream into jello mixture. Pour into a mold or deep dish, and chill overnight. Cut into squares and serve.

RED CABBAGE SALAD WITH BLUE CHEESE DRESSING

¼ cup distilled white or cider vinegar

2 pounds (about ½ large head) red cabbage, cored and thinly sliced

¼ pound bacon, cut into ½ inch dice

1 tablespoon butter

3 slices firm textured white bread, crusts removed, cut into ¼ inch dice

6 scallions, diced

2 tablespoons red wine vinegar

1 teaspoon Dijon mustard

1 tablespoon vegetable oil

¾ teaspoon salt

¼ teaspoon ground pepper

2 ounces blue cheese, preferably saga blue or Gorgonzola

Bring 4 quarts of water and the vinegar to a boil. Add the cabbage and blanch for 30 seconds. Drain in a colander and rinse under cold water until cool; drain and set aside.

Fry the bacon in a small skillet until brown and crisp. Pour the bacon and drippings into a small bowl and set aside.

In a large skillet, melt the butter over medium heat. When butter begins to foam, add bread cubes and sauté, tossing until brown, about 3 to 5 minutes. Drain on paper towels.

Add the red wine vinegar, mustard, oil, salt and pepper to the bacon drippings; stir until blended. Pour over the cabbage. Add scallions and blue cheese. Toss until well mixed. Sprinkle croutons over top. Serves 12.

MARINATED VEGETABLES

1 #2 can tiny English peas,
    drained

1 #2 can shoe peg corn, drained

Add:
½ cup chopped celery
½ cup chopped onion
½ cup chopped bell pepper

1 small jar chopped pimento,
    drained

Mix ¾ cup sugar, ½ cup cider vinegar, ½ cup oil, and salt to taste. Add veggies and marinate overnight.

STRAWBERRY SPINACH SALAD

2 pounds loose fresh spinach
1 quart fresh strawberries, halved
2 2-ounce packages slivered
    almonds, toasted

6 green onions, chopped
Poppy Seed Dressing

Remove stems from spinach; wash leaves thoroughly and pat dry or spin in salad spinner. Tear into bite sized pieces. Combine spinach with remaining ingredients except dressing; cover and chill.

Poppy Seed Dressing:
½ cup sugar
¼ cup apple cider vinegar
1 teaspoon finely chopped sweet
    onion

¼ teaspoon paprika
½ cup vegetable oil
1 tablespoon poppy seeds

Combine first 4 ingredients in processor. Process about 30 seconds or until well blended. With processor on high, gradually add oil in a slow stream through opening in lid until emulsified. Stir in poppy seeds.

Just before serving, pour Poppy Seed Dressing over salad; toss gently. Serves 12 to 14.

ASPARAGUS MOLD

1 cup all green canned asparagus
   (save liquid)
hot liquid
1 tablespoon gelatin, dissolved
   in ¼ cup cold water

½ cup mayonnaise
½ cup cream, whipped
1 teaspoon salt
2 tablespoons lemon juice
1 cup blanched almonds

Heat the liquid from the can of asparagus and pour over the dissolved gelatin. When partially set, fold in mayonnaise, whipped cream, and lemon juice. Add asparagus and almonds (cut in small pieces). Pour into mold and congeal. Serve with mayonnaise whipped with a little lemon juice and sprinkled with paprika. Serves 12.

BROCCOLI SALAD

1 bunch broccoli
⅓ cup raisins

¼ cup bacon pieces, cooked
¼ cup sunflower seeds

Separate broccoli into flowerets. Combine broccoli with remaining ingredients. Toss salad with salad dressing and refrigerate until serving.

Salad Dressing:
½ cup mayonnaise
1 teaspoon cider vinegar

1½ teaspoons sugar

Combine ingredients. Serves 4 to 6.

SHRIMP SALAD

6 cups cooked fresh peeled and
   deveined shrimp, coarsely
   chopped
1 cup celery, diced

juice of 1 lemon
salt and pepper to taste
¼ to ½ cup mayonnaise

Combine shrimp with celery and lemon juice. Add salt and pepper to taste. Add mayonnaise, just to coat mixture evenly. Chill, and serve over crisp bed of shredded lettuce. Serves 8 to 10.

CRAB SALAD

1 English cucumber, thinly sliced
⅓ cup celery, diced
½ cup thinly sliced onion rings

8 ounces lump white crab meat,
  drained and chilled
½ teaspoon salt
½ teaspoon black pepper

Vinaigrette:
½ cup raspberry vinegar
⅓ cup sugar

1 tablespoon teriyaki sauce

Toss vegetables with salt and pepper, refrigerate while mixing vinaigrette. Mix vinaigrette ingredients until sugar is dissolved and toss with vegetables and crab. Serve over crisp shredded lettuce with tomato wedges. Serves 4 to 6.

HOT CHICKEN SALAD

We wonder how much of this we have made for luncheon entrées!
Probably a ton!

4 cups cooked chicken breast,
  processed
3 cups cooked white rice
1½ cups shredded Cheddar cheese
1 cup celery, diced
¼ cup lemon juice

1 cup sliced water chestnuts
1 cup roasted sliced almonds
1 teaspoon salt
1 teaspoon pepper
1 to 1½ cups mayonnaise

Mix first 9 ingredients. Add just enough mayonnaise to bind. Press into greased 9 x 13 inch pan. Top with 1 package Ritz cracker crumbs mixed with ¼ cup melted butter. Bake at 350 degrees for 30 to 40 minutes until knife inserted in center comes out hot. Cut into squares. Serves 8 to 10.

CHICKEN-PASTA SALAD/FRUIT GARNISH

3 whole boneless chicken breasts,
   cooked and chopped
1 cup whole seedless green grapes
1 cup snow peas
12 spinach leaves, torn into pieces
1 large rib of celery with leaves,
   chopped
7 ounces cheese raviolini, cooked
1 6 ounce jar marinated artichoke
   hearts
1 kiwi, peeled and sliced

½ English cucumber, sliced
   (optional)
½ cup raisins
1 green onion, chopped
⅔ cup mayonnaise
½ cup freshly grated Parmesan
   cheese
⅓ cup fresh lemon juice
¼ cup orange juice
salt and ground pepper
mandarin orange sections

Combine first 11 ingredients in large serving bowl and toss gently. Mix mayonnaise, Parmesan cheese, lemon and orange juice, salt and pepper in small bowl until blended. Pour over chicken mixture, and blend carefully. Chill. Serve on bed of spinach leaves with mandarin orange sections as garnish. Serves 4.

ALMOND CHICKEN SALAD

A favorite in finger sandwiches for wedding receptions.

4 6-ounce boneless chicken breast
   halves, skin removed
½ cup diced celery
¼ cup roast almonds, sliced

½ teaspoon salt
½ teaspoon coarse ground pepper
½ cup mayonnaise
2 teaspoons fresh lemon juice

Steam or boil chicken breasts until done, and let cool. Place chicken in food processor, and pulse process until chicken is even in texture, leaving no large pieces, but not puréed. Mix together chicken and all other ingredients. More mayonnaise may be added if a creamier texture is desired. Serve on crisp leaf lettuce with tomato wedges. This is also great for stuffed tomatoes. Makes 6 to 8 servings.

CASHEW CHICKEN SALAD

½ cup wild rice, uncooked
1½ cups water
1 teaspoon salt
3 cups poached chicken, diced in
  1½ inch pieces
1 cup sliced mushrooms, sautéed
1 cup watercress leaves

½ cup diced celery
½ cup sliced green onion (tops
  only)
1 red bell pepper, thinly sliced in
  rings
1 cup chopped cashews

Dressing:
½ cup lite olive oil
⅓ cup white wine vinegar
1 tablespoon fresh tarragon,
  chopped

1 teaspoon salt
1 teaspoon freshly ground pepper
1 tablespoon sugar

Slowly add oil into vinegar using processor or wire whisk. Stir in remaining ingredients and set aside.

Bring water and salt to a boil in medium saucepan. Add rice. (Rinse first). Return to boil. Stir and reduce to simmer. Cover and cook for about 30 minutes until grains puff open. Rinse with cold water and drain well. Toss with remaining ingredients and dressing. Garnish with pepper rings. Chill ½ hour before serving. Serves 8 to 10.

HOT LEMON-GARLIC PASTA SALAD

2 tablespoons butter
2 tablespoons olive oil
6 cloves garlic, minced
⅓ cup fresh lemon juice
½ teaspoon salt
1 teaspoon freshly ground pepper

8 ounces linguine, cooked
⅓ cup chopped fresh parsley
½ cup thinly sliced green bell
  pepper
½ cup thinly sliced red pepper
1 cup sliced mushrooms, sautéed

Mix butter in saucepan on medium high heat. Add olive oil and garlic. Cook 1 minute stirring constantly. Add lemon juice, salt and pepper. Toss with pasta, mushrooms, peppers and parsley. Serve immediately. Serves 4.

BACON AND CHIVE POTATO SALAD

4 pounds big red potatoes
1 pound lean bacon, diced
1 cup diced onion
1 tablespoon garlic, minced
1 tablespoon sugar
¼ cup cider vinegar

¼ cup chicken stock
⅓ cup white wine
1 teaspoon salt
½ teaspoon freshly ground pepper
½ cup chopped fresh chives

Peel and boil potatoes just until tender. Drain and let cool enough to handle. Cut into ¼ inch slices, cover and set aside.

Cook bacon in skillet until crisp. Remove and drain well on paper towels. Cook garlic in drippings on medium low heat until tender. Add sugar and continue cooking for several minutes. Stir in vinegar, chicken stock and wine and simmer 2 more minutes. Add salt and pepper. Pour over warm potatoes and add chives and bacon. Toss gently and serve. Serves 8 to 10.

SHRIMP AND MUSHROOM SALAD

24 jumbo shrimp, peeled and
     deveined
24 snow peas
16 large white mushrooms, thinly
     sliced

½ cup pecans, chopped
3 tablespoons shallots, minced
8 leaves of green leaf lettuce

Vinaigrette:
2 tablespoons Dijon mustard
⅓ cup fresh lime juice
2 tablespoons freshly chopped dill

½ cup olive oil
½ cup corn oil
salt and pepper to taste

Cook shrimp just until pink. Drain. Cool and then refrigerate. Cut into 3 pieces. Blanch snow peas in salted boiling water for 2 minutes. Rinse with cold water and pat dry. Cut in half. Combine shrimp, peas, mushrooms, pecans, and shallots in large bowl. Add vinaigrette and toss. Serve on leaf lettuce and garnish with thinly sliced lime twist.

Vinaigrette: Combine mustard and lime juice. Add oils slowly, whisking well after each addition. Add chopped dill, then salt and pepper to taste. Serves 8.

POPPY SEED DRESSING FOR GREEN SALAD

⅔ cup honey
1 medium onion, grated
1 teaspoon salt
white pepper to taste

6 tablespoons French's mustard
¾ cup vinegar
3 or 4 tablespoons poppy seed
2 cups oil

Process first 6 ingredients. Slowly incorporate oil and add poppy seeds.

CREAMY ROQUEFORT DRESSING

1 cup sour cream
1 cup mayonnaise
6 ounces cream cheese, room
   temperature
½ teaspoon fresh lemon juice
   (do not substitute)

¼ teaspoon salt
⅛ teaspoon garlic juice
freshly ground black pepper
3 ounces Roquefort cheese,
   crumbled
milk

Blend all ingredients except cheese in processor until just smooth. Add cheese and process until just mixed. Makes approximately 3 cups.

PECAN DIP

½ small can frozen orange juice
1 cup ground pecans

1 8-ounce package cream cheese,
   at room temperature

Process cream cheese and juice. Stir in pecans. Great for fruit or pound cake.

SHRIMP SAUCE

1 pint mayonnaise
1 cup ketchup
⅔ cup horseradish
1 large onion, grated
1½ teaspoons salt

3 cloves garlic, grated
½ cup sherry
¼ cup lime juice
¼ cup lemon juice

Blend together in processor or mixer, chill and serve.

JOSEPHINE'S HOMEMADE MAYONNAISE

1 egg
2 cups Wesson or canola oil
1 teaspoon salt

juice of 1 lemon
2 teaspoons prepared mustard

Blend egg in processor until pale yellow. Slowly add oil in thin stream. Add other ingredients and process well.

MEEMAW'S SHRIMP COCKTAIL SAUCE

4 parts Bennett chili sauce to 1
   part ketchup (about 20 ounces
   to 5 ounces)
1 cup finely chopped celery
2 small onions, grated

Worcestershire sauce to taste
juice of ½ lemon
2 tablespoons mustard
horseradish to taste

Blend all and let mellow a few days before serving.

LORETTA'S BARBEQUE SAUCE

Cook until soft:

¼ cup **Wesson oil**
¾ cup **chopped onion**

1 clove **garlic, chopped**

Add:

1 cup **honey**
1 cup **ketchup**
½ cup **wine vinegar**
½ cup **Worcestershire sauce**
1 tablespoon **dry mustard**

1½ teaspoons **salt**
1 teaspoon **oregano**
1 teaspoon **black pepper**
½ teaspoon **thyme**

Simmer a few minutes. Great on pork.

MEEMAW'S SQUASH PICKLES

*We always had these during the summer with our
fresh vegetables, especially peas.*

8 cups **sliced yellow crookneck
  squash (the smaller the
  squash, the better)**
2 cups **sliced yellow onions**
¼ cup **salt**

3 cups **sugar**
2 cups **vinegar**
2 tablespoons **mustard seed**
2 tablespoons **celery seed**

Cover onion and squash with salt. Ice for 2 hours. Bring sugar, vinegar and seeds to boil and simmer for 10 minutes. Drain squash and add to vinegar mixture. Boil for 5 minutes. Put in sterile jars and seal. Chill before serving.

Morgon, Bob's grandson, picks figs for fig preserves.

$\mathcal{E}$ntrées

Living room before restoration, with all the cracks patched. (1989)

Shirley and John pressure wash house before grand opening. (1989)

BEST FRIED CHICKEN

8 6-ounce boneless, skinless,
   chicken breast halves
2 cups buttermilk

4 cups self rising flour
1 tablespoon coarse ground pepper
2 teaspoons salt

Soak chicken in buttermilk for 1 hour. Dredge in flour, patting to coat chicken well. Fry in skillet with vegetable oil, ½ inch deep, on each side until golden brown and crisp. Stand chicken on sides on paper towels to drain. This will prevent one side of chicken becoming soggy. Serve immediately. Serves 8.

CHICKEN CRÊPES

Shirley's creation—Another luncheon favorite.

12 6-inch crêpes

1 to 1½ cups Monterey Jack
   cheese, shredded

Sauce:
1 16-ounce can tomatoes, drained
1 4-ounces chopped green chili
   peppers

½ teaspoon ground coriander
½ teaspoon salt
1 cup sour cream

Place ingredients for sauce in blender and blend until smooth. Set aside.

Crêpe Mixture:
2 cups cooked chicken breast,
   finely chopped
1 3-ounce package cream cheese,
   softened

2 tablespoons sour cream
¼ cup onion, finely chopped
½ teaspoon salt
½ teaspoon pepper

Mix ingredients for crêpe mixture by hand. Spread mixture on crêpes and roll up. Place in buttered 13 x 9 inch baking dish, seam side down. Pour sauce over crêpes and cover with foil. Bake at 350 degrees for 20 minutes. Remove foil and cover with cheese. Return to oven, uncovered, until cheese melts. Serve immediately. Serves 6.

CHICKEN ALFREDO, MARTY STYLE

4 8-ounce boneless, skinless
   chicken breast halves
½ cup dry white wine (if you
   wouldn't drink it, don't use it)
1½ pints heavy whipping cream
1 teaspoon good olive oil (I like
   French olive oil best)
¼ cup minced shallot
½ cup grated Romano cheese
½ cup grated Parmesan cheese

16 ounces softened cream cheese,
   cut into ½ inch pieces
2 medium cloves of garlic, minced
   fine or pressed through garlic
   press
¼ teaspoon ground nutmeg
1 tablespoon fresh sweet basil,
   finely minced
salt and pepper to taste (you won't
   need much)
cooked linguine or angel hair pasta

Remove excess fat and any cartilage from chicken breast halves, and cut into bite sized pieces. Over medium heat, sauté shallots for about 2 or 3 minutes, and add garlic. Continue cooking until shallots have begun to turn transparent, but not browned. Be careful, the shallots will cook quickly. Add the cut chicken, and stir frequently until the chicken has been seared well on all sides. Be careful not to over cook the chicken at this point. It should only be seared, not cooked. Add the softened cream cheese and stir until evenly melted. Add the wine, and stir until combined with the cream cheese. Next, add the cream. Let the mixture cook until the chicken is tender, being careful not to over cook. Chicken should always be thoroughly cooked, but over-cooking will cause it to be dry and chewy. Cooking time will be about 20 minutes from the time that the cream comes to a medium simmer. DO NOT allow sauce to come to a boil. Add the nutmeg and basil after 15 minutes. If desired, fresh carrots which have been finely julienned, and then finely diced can be added to sauce after 10 minutes of cooking to add color; not more than a few tablespoons, though. The Romano and Parmesan go in just before the sauce is done, and the heat should be reduced to low to prevent the cheese from sticking to the bottom of the pot and burning. Stir constantly until the cheeses are completely melted and incorporated into the sauce. Add salt and pepper to taste. I find that very little, if any, salt is needed. Serve with cooked pasta. This will serve 6 to 8.

CHICKEN PANACHE

Our most popular dinner entrée.

8 6-ounce whole chicken breasts,
  boneless and skinless
8 strips lean, center cut bacon
8 slices corned beef, 1 ounce each,
  or 8 slices dried beef
16 jumbo mushrooms, sliced

1 leek, diced
1 stick butter
2 10¾-ounce cans mushroom soup
¾ cup sour cream
1 teaspoon black pepper
⅓ cup Marsala

Place 1 slice corned beef or dried beef on one side of each breast. Fold other side of breast over, sandwiching beef between breasts. Wrap one piece of bacon around each breast. Place in baking dish. Sauté mushrooms and leeks in butter for 5 minutes. Add remaining ingredients, stir and pour over chicken. Bake uncovered in a 250 degree oven for 4 hours. Serve with rice. Makes fabulous gravy. Serves 8.

BABY HOT BROWNS

This is an old Southern recipe.
It was a favorite in many diners throughout the South.

20 slices white bread
1 cup thick cheese sauce
1½ cups diced cooked chicken or
  turkey

½ cup freshly grated Parmesan
  cheese
3 slices bacon, broiled

Cut out bread rounds and brown on one side under broiler. Make cheese sauce and mix with meat. Spread the untoasted side with mixture (about 2 tablespoons on each). Sprinkle with Parmesan cheese and garnish with piece of bacon. Place on sheet and bake at 500 degrees until cheese melts.

Thick Cheese Sauce:
3 tablespoons butter
3 tablespoons flour
½ cup grated sharp Cheddar
  cheese

1 cup milk
salt, white pepper and cayenne to
  taste

Melt butter in double boiler. Add flour and blend. Add cheese, milk, and salt, white pepper and cayenne to taste. Makes 20 baby hot browns.

CHICKEN AND BROCCOLI PIE

2 recipes of Standard Pie Crust
(see index)
1 large onion, diced
1½ cups mushrooms, sliced
2 cups broccoli, cooked and
chopped
4 cups pulled chicken, cooked

2 cups chicken broth
½ cup cream
2 teaspoons salt
1 teaspoon pepper
6 tablespoons plain flour
1 stick butter

Melt butter in skillet. Cook onion and mushrooms until tender. Add flour and stir until blended. Slowly add chicken broth and cream. Cook over medium low heat; stirring constantly until thickened. Add salt and pepper.

Roll out a little over half of the pastry and line a 9 x 13 inch pan. Place chicken and then broccoli over pastry. Pour sauce over meat and vegetables. Roll out remaining pastry and top pie; sealing edges. Bake on lower shelf in 425 degree oven for 40 to 50 minutes or until pastry is nicely browned. Serves 8 to 10.

For a really old fashioned chicken pie, substitute 1 cup English peas and 1 cup cooked diced carrots instead of broccoli and mushrooms. Before topping pie with crust, drop 6 whole raw eggs one at a time evenly through pie.

EASY ALFREDO

4 8 ounce chicken breasts
3 cartons heavy whipping cream
½ cup freshly grated Parmesan
cheese

2 tablespoons minced garlic
2 teaspoons basil
1 stick butter
salt and pepper to taste

Cut chicken into ½ inch strips. Sauté in butter just until opaque in color. Add remaining ingredients and simmer on low heat for 15 minutes. Do not boil. Serve over your favorite pasta. I like angel hair or linguine. Serves 6 to 8.

CHICKEN COUNTRY CAPTAIN

An old Southern favorite.

8 6-ounce chicken breast halves, boneless, skinless
1 green bell pepper, diced in ½ inch pieces
1 red bell pepper, diced in ½ inch pieces
1 large onion, diced
8 ounces raisins
2 28-ounce cans diced tomatoes, with juice

1 cup water
2 teaspoons salt
1 teaspoon pepper
2 to 4 tablespoons curry powder, to taste
2 teaspoons thyme
1 tablespoon sugar
1 cup dry roasted peanuts, chopped for topping
chutney

Cut each breast into two strips. Dredge in plain flour seasoned with salt. Fry in vegetable oil until golden brown. Drain and set aside. Remove all but 2 tablespoons of oil from pan. Sauté peppers and onion in drippings for about 10 minutes on medium heat, stirring every minute or so. Cut chicken strips into bite size pieces and add to pepper and onion mixture with all other ingredients, except for peanuts and chutney. Stir well and place in covered baking pan. Bake in a 300 degree oven for 2 hours, stirring after 1 hour. Add water if mixture is too thick. Serve over white rice and top with peanuts, serving chutney on the side. This dish can be made the day before and tastes even better. Freezes well. Serves 10 to 12.

CHICKEN KABOB

4 8-ounce boneless chicken breasts

¼ cup sesame seed
8 6-inch skewers

Marinade:
½ cup soy sauce
¼ cup honey

1 teaspoon freshly grated ginger
1 teaspoon minced garlic

Soak skewers several hours to prevent burning. Cut each breast in two strips lengthwise. Soak in marinade 3 to 4 hours. Skewer one strip of chicken per skewer. Sprinkle with sesame seeds and grill over low heat about 3 minutes per side. **Do not overcook** or chicken will be dry. Serves 4 (2 kabobs each).

CHICKEN HASH

3 pounds chicken, rinsed and dried
1 large onion, quartered
2 ribs of celery, halved
1 bay leaf
¼ teaspoon dried red pepper flakes
6 scallions, sliced
½ stick butter
3 cooked boiling potatoes (about
    1½ pounds), cut into ½ inch
    cubes

¼ teaspoon dried sage, crumbled
    (optional)
1 teaspoon dried thyme, crumbled
    (optional)
pinch of cayenne
½ cup dry white wine
½ cup heavy cream

Cook chicken in water with onion, celery, bay leaf and pepper flakes. Let cool in liquid. Remove skin and bones and cube chicken. Strain liquid and reserve 2 cups.

In skillet over medium heat cook scallions in butter till soft; about 1 minute. Add potatoes, chicken, liquid, sage, thyme and cayenne. Cook 5 minutes. Add wine and cook stirring 5 minutes or until liquid is reduced to about ¼ cup. Add cream and cook stirring for 5 minutes. Serves 8.

CHICKEN PUDDING—1824

We found this recipe in an old book and it was dated 1824. It is typical of the creativity of cooks who worked with limited ingredients...good but simple.

Boil chicken in water, salt and pepper, parsley and thyme. Put chicken pieces, drained, in dish.

Pudding:
½ cup milk
3 tablespoons melted butter
3 eggs

½ cup flour and ½ cup flour
salt and pepper

Combine ingredients incorporating flour ½ cup at a time. Pour over chicken. Bake at 400 degrees until done, approximately 30 minutes.

CHICKEN BREAST SUPREME

6 whole boned and halved chicken breasts
3 cups sour cream
3 teaspoons celery salt
2 teaspoons paprika
½ teaspoon pepper
1 teaspoon salt

4 teaspoons Worcestershire sauce
2 tablespoons lemon juice (or ¼ cup)
2 cloves garlic, chopped
½ cup butter
½ cup Crisco
1¾ cups cracker or bread crumbs

Combine sour cream, lemon juice, Worcestershire sauce, celery salt, paprika, garlic, salt and pepper. Pour over chicken, coating each piece well. Marinate overnight in refrigerator.

Set oven to 350 degrees. Remove chicken from marinade and roll in crumbs. Arrange in baking dish in single layer. Melt butter and shortening in microwave. Spoon half butter mixture over chicken. Bake uncovered 45 minutes. Spoon balance over chicken and bake 10 to 15 minutes longer. Serve with small amount of white sauce (recipe below) and sprinkle with toasted sliced almonds. Yield 6 servings.

CHICKEN AND WILD RICE

1 6-ounce package long grain & wild rice
1 pint sour cream
1 10¾-ounce can mushroom soup
1 cup sliced mushrooms, sautéed

½ cup chopped black olives
¼ cup chopped pimento
3 cups diced cooked chicken
¼ cup sliced almonds

White Sauce:
2 tablespoons plain flour
2 tablespoons butter
1 cup milk

½ teaspoon salt
¼ teaspoon pepper

Melt butter in small sauce pot. Stir in flour and cook on low heat until it begins to bubble. Slowly add milk, using wire whip, and cook stirring constantly until sauce thickens. Add salt and pepper. Set aside. Cook rice according to package directions. Stir mushroom soup, mushrooms, olives and pimento into white sauce. In buttered casserole dish, alternate layers of rice, chicken and cream sauce mixture. Repeat layers ending with sauce. Top with almonds and bake at 350 degrees for 30 to 40 minutes. Serves 6 to 8.

GEORGIA PECAN CHICKEN

This recipe was shared with us by our local pecan distributor, Tucker Pecan Co.

3 cups plain flour
1 cup ground pecans
1 teaspoon salt
1 teaspoon pepper
6 teaspoons Dijon mustard

6 whole boneless, skinless chicken
   breasts
4 tablespoons butter
2 tablespoons Dijon mustard
½ cup heavy whipping cream

Mix first 4 ingredients in a bowl. Cut chicken breasts in half along seam creating 2 equal parts. Place a sheet of plastic wrap or wax paper over the chicken and pound with a mallet until each breast is about ⅛-inch thick. Remove paper and coat each breast with Dijon mustard, using about 1 teaspoon of mustard per breast half. Dredge coated breasts in flour mixture and shake off excess. Melt butter in a large sauté pan or skillet and cook chicken breasts over medium heat until golden brown on both sides. Remove the chicken and place on a warm plate. Pour off excess butter from the pan leaving browned crumb for flavor. Reduce heat to low and add 2 tablespoons Dijon mustard to the pan and mix with the leavings. Slowly add heavy whipping cream and stir constantly until sauce has been reduced to half the original volume. Arrange 2 chicken breasts on each plate and ladle sauce over them. Sprinkle pecan pieces for garnish.

SHRIMP NEW ORLEANS

4 pounds shrimp; raw, peeled and
   deveined
2 cloves garlic, minced
½ teaspoon paprika
1 cup butter, melted

⅓ cup chopped parsley
½ cup dry sherry
2 cups soft bread crumbs
½ to 1 teaspoon cayenne pepper

Place shrimp in baking dish. Toss rest of ingredients together. Spoon over top of shrimp. Bake at 325 degrees for 20 to 25 minutes. Serves 6 to 8.

PECAN CATFISH AND SWEET POTATO CHIPS

This recipe was shared with us by our local pecan distributor, Tucker Pecan Co.

1½ pounds catfish filets
2 tablespoons brown mustard
2 teaspoons honey
⅔ cup pecans and ⅓ cup seasoned
    bread crumbs, ground together

¾ pound sweet potatoes, thinly
    sliced
peanut oil
orange wedges

Cut catfish fillets into ½ x 2 inch fingers. Brush with mustard and honey. Dredge in the mixture of pecans and bread crumbs and set aside. Sauté sweet potatoes in peanut oil until crisp and brown; drain on paper towels. Add oil to pan and sauté fish until it flakes to the touch, 4 to 5 minutes per side. Serve fish with the chips and orange wedges. Serves 4.

COQUILLE ST. JACQUES

Shirley's son Ryan loves this seafood dish. It serves 6,
but only serves 2 when Ryan sits down.

6 tablespoons butter
3 tablespoons plain flour
1 teaspoon salt
¼ teaspoon white pepper
2 cups cream
½ pound scallops, sliced in half
    lengthwise
¼ cup onion, chopped

¾ cup mushrooms, sliced
½ pound large shrimp, cooked,
    peeled, deveined and sliced in
    half lengthwise
½ pound lump white crab meat
2 tablespoons sweet sherry
1 cup soft bread crumbs tossed
    with ¼ cup melted butter

Using a double boiler, melt 4 tablespoons of the butter. Blend in flour. Gradually add cream and cook, stirring constantly, over direct medium high heat until mixture begins to simmer. Meanwhile, start water boiling in bottom of double boiler. Place cream mixture over boiling water and cook 5 minutes longer, stirring constantly. Melt remaining butter in skillet. Add scallops, mushrooms and onions. Cook over medium heat just until scallops are opaque. Combine sauce, scallop mixture, shrimp, crab, sherry, salt and pepper. Mix and spoon into 6 ramekins and top with buttered bread crumbs. Bake in preheated 400 degree oven for 10 minutes or until lightly browned. Serve immediately; do not reheat as seafood will be tough and chewy.

SHRIMP RAMEKINS

¼ pound butter
2 pounds raw shrimp, peeled and
  deveined
1 10¾-ounce can mushroom soup
¼ pound cream cheese
1 cup sour cream
¼ teaspoon black pepper

2 teaspoons salt
½ teaspoon paprika
1 teaspoon Worcestershire sauce
⅛ teaspoon cayenne pepper
1 teaspoon parsley
½ cup Parmesan cheese, grated
2 tablespoons dry sherry

Melt butter in skillet; add shrimp and sauté for 2 minutes. Add mushrooms and cook slowly for several minutes turning frequently. Beat softened cream cheese and sour cream until light and creamy. Add creamed mixture slowly to shrimp and bring just to boiling. Add remaining ingredients except for cheese. Fill 6 to 8 ramekins and sprinkle with cheese. Place under broiler just until golden brown.

SHRIMP ETOUFFEE

1 stick butter
1 cup chili sauce
¼ cup chopped onion
¼ cup chopped celery
1 shallot, minced

1 teaspoon cayenne pepper, or to
  taste
1 teaspoon salt
½ cup dry white wine
2 pounds uncooked shrimp,
  shelled and deveined

Melt butter in large skillet over medium heat. Add onion, celery and shallots and sauté for 2 minutes. Add chili sauce, salt, cayenne and wine. Cook for 5 minutes. Add shrimp and cook just until pink. Do not over cook! Serve immediately over white rice. Garnish with sprig of parsley and lemon twist. Serves 4 to 6.

BAKED CRAB AND SHRIMP

1 medium green bell pepper,
   chopped
1 medium onion, chopped
1 cup celery, chopped
8 ounces white lump crab meat,
   flaked
8 ounces cooked shrimp, chopped

½ teaspoon salt
¼ teaspoon black pepper
1 teaspoon Worcestershire sauce
1 cup mayonnaise
1 tablespoons lemon juice
1 cup buttered bread crumbs

Combine ingredients, except bread crumbs. Place in buttered 8 x 8 inch baking dish and cover with buttered bread crumbs. Bake in 350 degree oven for 30 minutes. Serves 6.

PIQUANT DEVILED CRAB MEAT

1 pound lump crab meat
1 stick butter
3 tablespoons flour
¾ cup cream
½ cup buttered bread crumbs
¼ teaspoon cayenne pepper
½ teaspoon Worcestershire sauce

4 tablespoons cream sherry
3 tablespoons chopped parsley
¾ cup milk
1 small onion, diced
¾ teaspoon salt
1½ teaspoons dry mustard

Melt butter in sauce pan on medium heat. Sauté onions until tender. Blend flour, salt, mustard and cayenne in large bowl. Gradually stir in cream and milk until smooth. Add mixture to butter and onions. Over low heat, cook until sauce thickens, stirring constantly. Add Worcestershire, sherry and crab meat; stir gently. Pour mixture into individual ramekins. Sprinkle buttered bread crumbs over top. Bake in preheated 350 degree oven about 10 minutes or until crumbs are golden brown. Serves 4.

OYSTER CRAB CAKES

My mother, Dabbo, made these one Christmas. For once, we were glad a dish was prepared that no one would eat but the two of us. They are delicious!

2 tablespoons butter
½ cup shallots, finely minced
2 large eggs, slightly beaten
2 tablespoons fresh parsley,
    chopped
1 tablespoon jalapeño pepper,
    finely minced

1 teaspoon salt
½ teaspoon black pepper
2 tablespoons heavy cream
1 pound lump white crab meat
1½ cups soft white bread crumbs
3 dozen oysters, drained well
1 cup plain dry bread crumbs

Melt butter in skillet over medium heat. Add shallots and cook until tender. Combine eggs, parsley, jalapeño, salt, pepper and cream in large bowl. Stir in shallots and crab. Toss with soft bread crumbs. Spread 1 tablespoon crab mixture into palm of hand. Place 1 oyster on top and pat mixture around oyster. Gently pat dry bread crumbs on each cake coating all sides. Flatten slightly and place on baking pan generously greased with butter. Refrigerate 3 to 4 hours. Bake in preheated 450 degree oven on middle rack for 5 minutes. Turn each cake over gently and bake for 5 more minutes. Sprinkle with lemon juice or favorite hot sauce and serve. Serves 12.

CRAB PIE

1 9-inch pie shell
2 cups lump white crab meat,
    flaked
1 cup sliced mushrooms
2 tablespoons shallots, minced
¾ cup Provolone cheese, grated

3 eggs
1 cup heavy cream
2 teaspoons Crazy Jane salt
1 teaspoon black pepper
2 tablespoons Madeira wine

Sauté mushrooms and shallots. Drain and flake crab. Toss mushrooms, shallots, crab, cheese, salt and pepper together. Whisk together eggs, cream and Madeira. Put mushroom/crab mixture into pie shell. Top with egg mixture. Bake at 350 degrees for 40 to 45 minutes. Cool for 10 minutes before serving. Serves 6.

CRAB CAKES

1 pound lump white crab meat	¼ cup plain dry bread crumbs
1 small red pepper, minced	1 tablespoon Worcestershire
1 celery stalk, minced	2 tablespoons heavy cream
1 small onion, grated	½ teaspoon hot pepper sauce
2 eggs, slightly beaten	2 sticks butter
juice of 1 lemon	2 tablespoons olive oil

Pick over crab to remove any shell or cartilage. Combine all ingredients and mix well. If mixture is not moist enough to form cakes, add a little mayonnaise. A little Dijon mustard can be added to mixture for an extra zip. Form about 4 tablespoons into a patty. Roll in white corn meal. Melt butter and olive oil together in heavy skillet over medium high heat. Fry crab cakes on each side until golden brown. Drain; sprinkle with lemon juice and serve hot. Makes 8 patties; 4 servings.

These are a big hit made bite size as appetizers. Recipe will make 40 to 50.

CRAB SOUFFLÉ

This recipe was shared with us by a neighbor and friend, Ruth McLemore, a truly wonderful Southern cook. We have used it for many luncheons.

1 pound crab meat, fresh or canned	16 slices white bread
1 cup diced celery	1 pound Cheddar cheese, grated
2 tablespoons prepared mustard	2 cups milk, scalded and cooled
½ cup mayonnaise	4 eggs, beaten
	paprika, salt and pepper, to taste

Combine crabmeat, celery, paprika, mustard and mayonnaise to make filling. Prepare 8 sandwiches; cut crust from bread. In a buttered 13 x 9 x 2 inch pan, layer a row of sandwiches and ½ the cheese. Place second row of sandwiches in dish, not directly on top of first layer. Cover with remaining cheese. Beat eggs, salt and pepper into scalded milk. Pour over sandwiches, cover, and refrigerate overnight. Place casserole in pan of water. Sprinkle paprika on top. Bake at 325 degrees for 30 minutes. Yield 8 servings.

SALMON LOAF

1 egg
⅔ cup evaporated milk
2 cups canned pink salmon,
    drained
1 cup bread crumbs
1 teaspoon grated lemon rind

1 minced small onion
½ teaspoon salt (Crazy Jane)
⅛ teaspoon pepper
2 tablespoons butter, melted
2 teaspoons lemon juice
1 small jar capers, drained

Beat egg; add milk. Flake salmon into egg mixture; add bread crumbs, rind, onion, salt and pepper, mixing well. Add butter and lemon juice. Spoon into greased 9 x 5 inch loaf pan; bake at 350 degrees for about 50 minutes or until firm. Yield 4 servings.

CATFISH CROQUETTES

3 pounds catfish nuggets or filets
¾ cup celery, finely diced
½ cup onion, finely diced
1 teaspoon salt
1 teaspoon black pepper

3 eggs, slightly beaten
¼ cup cream
1 tablespoon lemon juice
1 cup plain dry bread crumbs

Steam catfish, cool. Flake or pulse in processor. Add all ingredients and mix well with hands. Form croquettes with about ½ cup mixture each. Coat each with white corn meal. Fry in ½ inch deep vegetable oil on each side until golden brown. Drain on paper towels and serve immediately. Serve with tartar or cocktail sauce. Makes about 8 croquettes.

TARTAR SAUCE

2 cups real mayonnaise
2 tablespoons fresh lemon juice
1 small onion, grated

½ cup dill pickle relish
1 teaspoon Krazy Jane salt
½ teaspoon black pepper

Mix all ingredients. Let chill for several hours.

SHRIMP AND EGGPLANT EXTRAVAGANZA

1 large eggplant, unpeeled
24 jumbo shrimp, cooked, peeled
   and deveined

1 cup self-rising cornmeal
1 teaspoon salt

Sauce:
2 cups half and half
4 tablespoons plain flour
4 tablespoons butter
1 teaspoon salt

½ to 1 teaspoon cayenne pepper
1 tablespoon fresh lemon juice
½ cup shredded sharp Cheddar
   cheese

Melt butter in medium saucepan on medium low heat. Sprinkle flour over butter and stir. Slowly add half and half and stir constantly on medium low heat until thickened. Add remaining sauce ingredients and stir until cheese is melted. Next, cut top off of eggplant. Slice ½ inch off two sides of eggplant (opposite sides). Slice eggplant into 4 equal slices lengthwise. Dip in water and coat with cornmeal-salt mixture. Fry in vegetable oil turning once until golden brown on each side. Drain on paper towels. Put shrimp into cheese sauce for a few minutes just until they are warm. Pour about ½ cup sauce and 6 shrimp over each slice of eggplant. With a side salad, this is a meal in itself. Serves 4.

SAUTÉED SALMON FILETS

4 6-ounce Norwegian salmon
   filets, at least ¾ inch thick
8 ounces sliced mushrooms
½ cup leeks, diced

¼ cup lemon juice
2 teaspoons Crazy Jane salt
4 tablespoons butter
2 tablespoons capers

Sauté mushrooms and leeks in butter until tender. Add lemon juice, Crazy Jane and capers. Remove skin from filets, if any, and marinate salmon in mushroom mixture for 1 hour. Remove salmon and drain juices from marinade. Sauté salmon in skillet with 2 tablespoons melted butter and 1 tablespoon olive oil on medium heat for about 3 minutes on each side, or desired doneness. Remove salmon from skillet and add mushroom mixture and stir fry for a couple of minutes until hot. Serve over salmon with lemon twist and sprig of dill. Serves 4.

DABBO'S MEATLOAF

2 pounds ground chuck (extra lean beef makes a hard, dry meatloaf)
½ cup diced celery
½ cup diced onion
½ cup grated carrot
2 large eggs, beaten

1 cup dry bread crumbs
½ cup ketchup
¼ cup Worcestershire sauce
2 teaspoons salt
1 teaspoon pepper
4 slices bacon

Topping:
1 cup ketchup
¼ cup Worcestershire sauce

½ cup honey

Mix all ingredients well with hands. Shape into a loaf 2½ inches high. Place in a baking dish and pat to remove any cracks. Lay the slices of bacon evenly over the loaf. Bake at 350 degrees for 45 minutes. Remove from oven and cover with topping, then bake for an additional 15 minutes. Serves 6 to 8.

GRITS AND GRILLADES

Great brunch dish — filling!

2½ inch thick slices top round steak (about 1½ pounds)
1½ teaspoons salt
¾ teaspoon black pepper
⅛ teaspoon red pepper flakes
4 cloves garlic, minced
2 tablespoons flour
2 tablespoons butter, melted

1 cup chopped sweet onion (preferably Vidalia)
½ cup chopped celery
½ cup chopped green pepper
1 16-ounce can tomatoes, drained
pinch sugar
1 cup water
2 cups regular grits, cooked

Pound steak to ¼ inch with mallet. Cut steak into 2 inch squares. In a Dutch oven heat ¼ cup bacon grease or oil over medium heat. Add meat and fry until browned. (Drain grease, keeping dregs.) Transfer to plate and set aside. To the Dutch oven add the butter and flour, stirring until roux is dark brown. To the roux add the onion, celery, bell pepper, and garlic and sauté until soft. Add tomatoes, sugar, and red pepper flakes and cook 3 minutes. Add water and stir well. Add meat to the pot. Add salt and pepper to taste. Tabasco may be added if desired. Lower heat and cook. Stir frequently. Cook about 2 hours. Serve over grits. Note: This dish is best if the grillades are cooled, refrigerated overnight, and reheated before serving. Serves 4.

SOUTHERN FRIED PORK CHOPS

Shirley's husband John worships these. He actually ate 3 one night and they are huge. But, then again, he's eaten 14 drumsticks in one night before.

6 1¼-inch thick center cut pork
   chops
1 cup plain flour seasoned with 1
   teaspoon salt and 1 teaspoon
   black pepper

2 medium onions, sliced
10 large white mushrooms, sliced
   thick
3 chicken bouillon cubes
½ cup sour cream

Dredge chops in flour. Brown on both sides in large skillet in small amount of vegetable oil on medium heat. Remove from skillet. Spoon remaining oil from skillet being careful to leave browned drippings. Place chops back in skillet with onions and mushrooms on top. Cover with water and add bouillon cubes, 1 teaspoon salt and pepper. Cover with lid and simmer on low heat for 1½ hours. Remove chops and thicken if necessary. Whisk in sour cream and add more salt if desired. If thickening is necessary, 2 to 4 tablespoons of plain flour whisked with ½ to ¾ cup water should be plenty. Put chops back in skillet to coat with gravy or place on platter and pour gravy over chops. Serve with mashed potatoes or rice. Gravy is fabulous. Serves 6.

SWEDISH MEATBALLS

1½ cups soft bread crumbs
¾ cup milk
3 tablespoons onion, finely
   chopped
4 tablespoons butter
1 pound lean ground beef
¼ teaspoon nutmeg

1½ teaspoons salt
½ teaspoon black pepper
1 tablespoon chopped mint leaves
1 egg, slightly beaten
½ cup plain flour
½ cup cream
½ cup chicken broth

Soak bread crumbs in milk. Sauté the onion in 2 tablespoons of the butter until soft.; add to bread crumbs, beef, seasonings and egg. Mix well and form into 1 inch balls. Roll in flour and brown in remaining 2 tablespoons butter. Add stock, cream and mint leaves and simmer gently for 10 minutes. Remove meatballs and thicken gravy with paste made of 2 tablespoons flour and 2 tablespoons cold water. Add paste to simmering gravy and stir constantly with wire whip until thickened. Place meatballs back in gravy and simmer for 5 more minutes. If thinner gravy is desired, add additional cream or chicken stock. Serve over rice. Serves 6 to 8.

ZESTY MEATBALLS

1 cup chopped onions	4 whole black peppercorns
½ cup green pepper, very finely diced	4 whole cloves
	1 bay leaf
2 beaten eggs	2 tablespoons lemon juice
1 2-ounce can anchovy fillets	4 tablespoons all-purpose flour
5 slices dry white bread	1 lemon, finely sliced
1 cup milk	2 tablespoons capers, drained
¾ cup water	1 pound ground beef
¾ cup dry white wine	½ pound ground veal
1½ teaspoons salt	½ pound ground pork
¼ teaspoon ground pepper	hot cooked noodles
2 tablespoons butter	snipped parsley

Soak anchovies in cold water for 20 to 25 minutes to remove excess salt; drain. Soak bread in milk. Sauté onions in butter until transparent, being careful not to let them brown. Combine anchovies, onion, eggs, bread mixture, salt, and pepper in a large mixing bowl. Add meats and mix well. Form meat mixture into balls approximately 1½ inches in diameter. It should yield about 2 dozen meatballs. In a large skillet mix the wine, cloves, bay leaf, water, lemon juice and peppercorns. Bring mixture to a simmer, and add meatballs. Cover and simmer 25 to 30 minutes. Remove meatballs and strain remaining liquid, returning it to the skillet and continuing to simmer. Mix ½ cup cold water into flour, dissolving flour completely. Stir flour mixture into simmering liquid, stirring constantly. Cook and stir until liquid is thick and bubbly. Add lemon slices, capers, and salt. Cook for 1 or 2 minutes longer. Place hot, cooked noodles on a platter, and top with meatballs. Pour the sauce over the meatballs and noodles, garnishing with parsley. Serves 6 to 8.

TOMATO CHEESE BURGER PIE

2 teaspoons minced onion
1 cup sifted flour
¼ cup cold water

½ teaspoon salt
⅓ cup shortening

Hamburger Filling:
¼ cup ketchup
1 teaspoon salt
¼ teaspoon marjoram
1 pound ground beef
1 beaten egg
½ cup bread crumbs
2 teaspoons minced onion

½ teaspoon sweet basil
⅛ teaspoon pepper
1 cup shredded Cheddar cheese
6 tomato slices or 3 canned
    tomatoes
6 slices cheese

Soak minced onion in water. Sift flour with salt into mixing bowl. Cut in shortening, and sprinkle with onion-water mixture, stirring with a fork until dough is moist enough to hold together. Roll out dough to fit an 8 or 9 inch pan.

Hamburger filling: Combine ketchup, minced onion, salt and herbs. Cook ground beef until it loses red color, remove from heat, and drain. Stir in ketchup mixture, cheese, egg and bread crumbs. Turn into pastry-lined pan. Top with tomato slices. Bake at 400 degrees 20 to 25 minutes, until crust is golden brown. Top with cheese. Bake 1 minute, or until cheese is softened. Serve hot. Recipe serves 6.

BEEF TENDERLOIN WITH MUSHROOM SAUCE

This is Barbara's son, Brad McCorvey's, favorite!
Shirley has to slap his hands when she's carving the loin. He laps up the scraps.

4 pound tenderloin, side muscle,
    fat and silver removed
1 pound sliced mushrooms
1 leek, diced
1 stick butter

2 large bay leaves
1 tablespoon Crazy Jane salt
1 teaspoon coarse black pepper
½ cup Marsala

Rub tenderloin with olive oil and 1 teaspoon salt. Sear on grill. Sauté mushrooms, leeks, pepper, and Crazy Jane in butter. Add bay leaves and Marsala; simmer for 5 minutes. Pour over tenderloin and marinate for 1 hour. Cook, uncovered, in 350 degree oven, with marinade covering tenderloin for 45 minutes. Meat should be medium depending on weight of tenderloin and oven variations. Remove meat and bay leaves. Pour mushroom mixture and drippings into small sauce pot. Make paste with 3 tablespoons flour and ½ cup water; add to simmering mixture and cook until thickened. Taste to adjust seasonings; add water or beef broth if thinner gravy is desired. Slice tenderloin, place on platter and cover with sauce. Serves 10.

BEEF TENDERLOIN KABOBS

1 4-pound beef tenderloin
¼ cup dark soy sauce
¼ cup olive oil

salt
coarse ground pepper

Remove fat and side muscle from tenderloin. Trim silver. Your butcher will do this for you. Rub generously with salt, pepper, and olive oil. Cut in half lengthwise. Next cut tenderloin into 2 inch pieces. Toss with soy sauce. Skewer meat with favorite vegetables and grill over medium coals. Cook until desired doneness. Be sure you soak skewers for several hours before using to keep them from burning. Serves 6 to 8.

BAKED HAM WITH PEAR PURÉE

1 10-pound precooked ham	¾ cup water
3 cups dry red wine	¾ cup sugar
6 pounds pears, peeled, cored and sliced ¼ inch thick	1 tablespoon grated fresh ginger
	2 teaspoons cornstarch

Trim fat on ham down to ¼ inch. Put ham on a rack in a large roasting pan. Slash patterns into fat. Pour 2 cups of wine over ham. Bake in 350 degree oven, basting every 15 minutes with pan juices. Add water as needed if liquid evaporates too quickly. Bake about 10 to 12 minutes per pound until internal temperature of ham reaches 140 to 150 degrees.

Pear Purée: Put pears, remaining wine, water, sugar and ginger in large aluminum pot. Bring to simmer and cook until soft, about 30 minutes. Process and return to pot. Continue cooking on low heat, about 30 minutes, stirring frequently until purée has reduced by ⅓. When ham is done, remove to serving platter and let stand 20 to 30 minutes. Meanwhile, skim fat from drippings. Mix cornstarch with 1 tablespoon water. Add to pan juices and cook over medium heat, stirring until smooth. Add more cornstarch if needed. Carve ham in thin slices and drizzle with gravy. Serve pear purée on the side.

Canned pears may be used if not in season. Purée 4 pounds canned pears. Add wine and ginger. Place in pot and cook over low heat stirring frequently until mixture has reduced, about 30 minutes. Taste and add a little sugar if desired. Serves 10 to 12.

MOM'S RED BEANS AND RICE

This recipe was shared with us by one of our clients. We love it!

1 pound dried red beans
4 quarts water
¾ cup chopped onion
¾ cup chopped celery
¾ cup chopped green peppers
2 teaspoons minced garlic
½ cup butter or margarine
2 to 3 large bay leaves
2 teaspoons salt

2 teaspoons paprika
1 teaspoon thyme
½ teaspoon ground red pepper
½ teaspoon oregano
1½ to 2 pounds sausage cut in
    thin slices
½ cup chopped parsley
Tabasco sauce (optional)

Let beans soak overnight or bring to a boil, cover and let sit 2 hours. Bring water to boil, add beans, reduce heat to medium and cook, uncovered, 1½ to 2 hours. Stir occasionally. While beans are cooking, sauté onion, celery, green peppers and garlic in butter in skillet until tender, about 10 minutes. Mix spices and add to sautéed veggies. Add bay leaf and parsley and sautéed veggies to beans.

Slice sausage and cook 20 minutes in 350 degree oven or about 10 minutes in microwave. Drain off fat and add to beans. Cook on low heat until ready to serve or beans become soft. Remove bay leaves before serving. Serve over cooked rice. Serves 8 to 10.

CURRY RIPE OLIVE SANDWICH

2 cups chopped ripe olives
    (2 7-ounce cans)
1 cup sliced green onions and tops
3 cups grated Colby cheese
    (1½ pounds)

1 cup mayonnaise
½ teaspoon salt
½ teaspoon curry powder
6 English muffins, split and
    toasted

Mix all ingredients and spread on muffin halves. Broil until cheese melts. May be cut in wedges for appetizer servings. Serves 6.

BROILED QUAIL WITH MUSTARD BUTTER AND WILD RICE PANCAKES

Another recipe shared by the same wine rep.

¼ pound unsalted butter, melted
4 tablespoons Dijon mustard
2 teaspoons wild honey
1 tablespoon roasted garlic
1 teaspoon minced fresh savory or
   oregano
2 teaspoons fresh lemon juice

8 boned quail
salt and freshly ground black
   pepper to taste
⅓ cup Sauvignon Blanc or
   Chardonnay
⅔ cup rich quail or chicken stock

Garnish:
Wild Rice Pancakes (recipe
   follows)

roasted wild mushrooms
watercress sprigs

Combine the butter, mustard, honey, garlic, savory, and lemon juice and slather over quail. Season lightly with salt and pepper. Marinate for at least 4 hours refrigerated.

Remove quail from the marinade and place breast side down in a broiler pan. Reserve marinade. Preheat the boiler to high heat. Broil the birds for 3 to 4 minutes. Turn over, paint with the marinade mixture, and broil for 3 minutes more or until the quail are golden brown, but still juicy. Remove and keep warm.

Add wine, stock, and remaining marinade to the broiler pan juices and reduce quickly to a light sauce consistency over high heat. Whisk constantly. Correct seasonings.

To roast garlic: Cut off top quarter of garlic head and drizzle with the olive oil, salt and pepper. Wrap securely in foil and bake in a 325 degree oven for 30 to 40 minutes or until garlic is very soft and creamy.

Wild Rice Pancakes: Prepare your favorite wild rice by package directions. Add 1 beaten egg and 4 sliced scallions to 2 cups cooled rice. Drop by tablespoons onto greased skillet. Turn when browned. Serves 4.

BARBARA'S DOVES

Every year we prepare a big game dinner from the bounty and hunting skills of Dr. Chuck Fletcher and Mr. Bobby Baird. We cook for about four days. The proceeds from the game dinner benefit our local children's home, "Brantwood". These two recipes were shared with us by Barbara Montoya, whose husband Ed is the director of "Brantwood".

12 doves, breast only
¼ cup butter
juice from 2 lemons
⅓ cup Worcestershire sauce

1 large onion, thinly sliced into rings
2 cups rosé wine
1 clove garlic, finely chopped

Wash doves and wipe with a clean, damp cloth or paper towels. Melt butter in large iron skillet, add garlic. Brown doves in skillet. Add all other ingredients. Cover and bake at 325 degrees till birds are tender. Yield 4 servings.

QUAIL WITH MUSHROOMS AND WHITE WINE

See above note regarding another Barbara Montoya recipe.

8 quail
8 slices of bacon
1 tablespoon butter
1 cup dry white wine

1 pound fresh mushrooms, cleaned
2 tablespoons lemon juice
wild rice

Prepare quail. Wrap a slice of bacon around each bird, securing with toothpicks. Place in small, buttered roasting pan, breast up. Cover and bake at 350 degrees for 30 minutes. Combine lemon juice and wine and pour over birds. Add mushrooms. Cover and bake 15 minutes more. Remove cover and baste frequently for 15 minutes. Spoon the liquid and mushrooms over the quail and serve with hot wild rice. Yield 4 servings.

SOUTHERN QUICHE

1 9-inch pie shell
1 cup ham, pulsed in processor
1½ cups Jarlsberg cheese, grated
1 small onion, diced

3 eggs
1 cup heavy cream
½ teaspoon fresh ground black
   pepper

Sauté ham and onion until onion is transparent. Drain well on paper towels. Beat eggs, cream and pepper. Sprinkle ham mixture and then cheese into pie shell. Pour egg mixture over ham and cheese. Bake at 350 degrees for 30 to 40 minutes until set. Cool 15 minutes before cutting. Serves 6.

HEARTY STUFFED SQUASH

6 medium yellow squash
2 medium zucchini, chopped
1 pound lean ground beef
½ cup cooked white rice

1 medium onion, diced
1 medium bell pepper, diced
1 teaspoon salt
1 tablespoon chopped fresh mint

Hollow out uncooked squash, reserving pulp. Combine ground beef, rice, onion, green pepper, cinnamon, salt and mint. Stuff into each squash and place in large pot. Cover with following ingredients :

1 28-ounce can diced tomatoes
   with juice
reserved pulp from squash
zucchini
2 teaspoons salt

1 teaspoon black pepper
juice of 1 lemon
2 tablespoons brown sugar
2 large bay leaves
any meat mixture left over

Toss ingredients and cover squash. Simmer, covered for 45 minutes to 1 hour. Remove bay leaves and serve tomato mixture over additional rice. Mixture can be thickened if desired. Serves 6.

MARINATED LOIN OF VENISON ROASTED WITH MUSTARD

This recipe was shared with us by one of our wine reps. Yummy!

1 5-pound loin of venison, well
  trimmed

Marinade:

2 tablespoons fruity olive oil
3 medium carrots
1 large yellow onion
2 whole shallots
3 large cloves garlic
5 cups hearty red wine

½ cup red wine vinegar
4 whole bay leaves
6 parsley stalks
16 whole juniper berries
2 teaspoons sea salt
12 whole black peppercorns

Mustard Coating:

3 large cloves garlic
⅓ cup chopped green onion
⅓ cup dry white wine
1 teaspoon each fresh sage and
  thyme or ½ teaspoon dried

1 cup Dijon mustard
¼ cup olive oil
1 teaspoon sea salt

Garnish:

Zinfandel reduction sauce and
  roasted wild mushrooms

Roughly chop the marinade vegetables and sauté in oil until lightly browned. Add the wine vinegar and remaining seasonings and bring to a boil. Reduce heat and simmer for 10 minutes and then cool before using.

For the mustard coating, place all ingredients in a food processor or blender and quickly process until smooth. Mixture should be very thick. Cover and refrigerate.

In a non-aluminum pan, pour the cooled marinade over the loin and marinate covered in the refrigerator for up to 24 hours. (We recommend at least 24 hours). Turn occasionally. Remove from the marinade, pat dry and quickly sear the meat in a hot sauté pan or on a grill (we prefer grill). If you don't have enough room, cut the loin in half and sear in two pieces.

(Continued on page 89)

(Continued from page 88)

Place loin in a roasting pan on a rack and coat well with the mustard coating. Roast in preheated 375 degree oven for 15 to 20 minutes or until meat is rare to medium rare. (Do not overcook). Allow the meat to rest at least 5 minutes before slicing.

Serve on warm plates with a reduction sauce made from rich game stock and zinfandel and roasted wild mushrooms. Serves 8 to 10.

EGGS BENEDICT/DIXIE STYLE

4 rounds Canadian bacon or
    Smithfield Virginia ham
2 large green tomatoes
½ cup cornmeal
ground black pepper and salt, to
    taste
4 English muffins, toasted

1½ cups whipping cream
1 tablespoon minced fresh thyme
    or basil
1 medium lemon
4 tablespoons butter
8 eggs, poached

Cut ham into rounds. Cut tomatoes into 8 (½ inch) thick slices. Dredge in cornmeal mixed with salt and pepper. Fry in melted butter until golden on both sides. Drain on paper towels and set aside. Put cream and herbs into small saucepan, boil gently until reduced to 1 cup. Remove from heat, add ½ teaspoon pepper and 2 tablespoons lemon juice; cover and set aside. Toast muffins under broiler till golden brown. Poach eggs.

Put 2 muffin halves on each warm plate. Top with ham, fried green tomato and egg. Spoon sauce over eggs and serve immediately. Garnish with a sprig of fresh thyme or basil. Yield 4 servings.

BARBARA'S SPINACH AND BACON QUICHE

Barbara served this every Friday in the little deli in the back of her Swiss Colony cheese and wine shop. The mall employees always looked forward to Friday.

Into a bowl mix:

2 eggs
1 carton whipping cream
1 teaspoon salt

½ teaspoon fresh ground black
    pepper

Add:

5 strips cooked, crumbled lean
    bacon
1 8-ounce package spinach,
    thawed and squeezed of as
    much liquid as possible

1¾ cups grated Jarlsberg or baby
    Swiss cheese

Add:
about ¼ cup half & half

Blend all well. Pour into 9-inch deep dish pie crust that has been fluted and pre-baked for 8 to 10 minutes in a 400 degree oven. Bake at 400 degrees for 15 minutes. Reduce heat to 350 degrees and bake 30 more minutes until just set. (Quiche will continue setting after removal from oven). Let set about 15 to 20 minutes before cutting. Warms great in microwave. Serves 6 people.

PIRATES COVE HAMBURGER SAUCE

Gulf Shores and Perdido Bay are Alabama's jewels. The beaches are snow white and the waters Caribbean azure. One of the places you must visit is Pirate's Cove. Their hamburgers and sauce make your heart sing.

1 tablespoon mayonnaise
1 tablespoon ketchup
1 tablespoon prepared mustard
1 tablespoon horseradish

1 teaspoon gin
1 teaspoon vermouth
1 tablespoon light Karo syrup
1 tablespoon sweet pickle relish

Mix all ingredients and spread on hamburgers. Yield 4 servings.

*The Cottage
- circa 1939 -
Bob and Barbara
restored.*

$\mathcal{V}$egetables

*Cottage before
renovation.*

*Cottage was a little
overgrown, don't
you agree?*

AUNT DOT'S ASPARAGUS CASSEROLE

1 large can green asparagus tips
2 cups heavy white sauce
2 hard cooked eggs, sliced

2 cups grated sharp cheese
1 cup bread crumbs

Arrange half the asparagus in a greased casserole. Place slices from one egg in a layer over the asparagus. Sprinkle with half of the cheese, and cover with one cup of the white sauce. Make the second layer the same as the first, and sprinkle with bread crumbs. Bake at 350 degrees for abut 20 minutes. Serves 6.

CABBAGE PIE

1 medium head cabbage, shredded
16 soda crackers
1 stick butter
4 tablespoons flour

½ teaspoon pepper
2½ teaspoons celery seed
2 cups milk

Alternate layers of cabbage and crushed crackers ending with crackers. You should have 3 layers. Make the white sauce, adding salt, pepper and celery seed. Pour over cabbage and crackers, and bake at 350 degrees for one hour. Serves 6.

MARINATED VEGETABLES

1 #2 can tiny English peas,
    drained
1 #2 can shoe peg corn, drained
½ cup chopped celery
½ cup chopped onion
½ cup chopped bell pepper

1 small jar chopped pimento
¾ cup sugar
½ cup cider vinegar
½ cup oil
salt to taste

Combine sugar, vinegar, oil, and salt. Add vegetables and marinate overnight. Serves 6.

SWEET POTATO SOUFFLÉ

2 cups cooked, mashed sweet
   potatoes
¾ cup hot milk
⅓ cup butter
lemon zest

1 teaspoon vanilla
¼ teaspoon salt
½ cup brown sugar
3 egg whites, stiffly beaten

Add butter and hot milk to mashed sweet potatoes; beat until fluffy. Add lemon zest, salt, and sugar. Fold in egg whites, beaten stiff but not dry. Pile lightly into a greased casserole. Bake in a 400 degree oven 30 to 35 minutes or until puffy and browned. Makes about 6 servings.

MA'S SWEET POTATO SOUFFLÉ

Our friend Benny Pasquariello from Washington, D.C. said he must have died and gone to heaven every time he ate this dish.

4 medium sized sweet potatoes
½ stick butter
3 eggs
1 cup sugar

1 cup evaporated milk
1 tablespoon lemon juice
1 teaspoon vanilla
1 teaspoon pumpkin pie spice

Boil sweet potatoes; peel and mash. Add butter, eggs, sugar, evaporated milk, lemon juice, vanilla, and pumpkin pie spice. Place in greased casserole and bake at 375 degrees until firm. Top with topping and return to oven until brown.

Topping:
1 cup chopped pecans
¼ cup brown sugar

¼ cup melted butter

Mix all ingredients together. Place on casserole.

SWEET POTATO CROQUETTES

3 cups sweet potatoes, cooked and
    mashed
¼ cup butter
1 teaspoon salt
4 tablespoons brown sugar

½ teaspoon cinnamon
½ cup shredded coconut
3 cups corn flakes, crushed
½ cup crushed pineapple, drained
1 egg

Combine all ingredients except corn flakes. Shape into balls about 1½ inches in diameter. Roll in egg and corn flakes. Fry in vegetable oil heated to 375 to 385 degrees until browned. Drain on paper towels. Makes about 6 servings.

SWEET POTATO TIMBALES

1 medium sweet potato (about ½
    pound)
2 tablespoons butter
2 eggs

¾ cup half & half
1 tablespoon flour
½ teaspoon salt

Peel and coarsely shred sweet potato. In saucepan over medium heat, cook sweet potato in butter until tender, about 10 minutes. Remove from heat. In medium bowl, mix eggs, half and half, flour and salt. Stir in sweet potato. Spoon potato mixture into 5 (6 ounce) molds sprayed with veggie cooking spray. Cook in water bath in 370 degree oven 15 to 20 minutes. Cool 5 minutes. Unmold and serve. Yield 5 (6 ounce) molds.

STEWED OKRA & TOMATOES

Place 2 cups okra cut in rounds and one diced onion in skillet with 1 stick butter. Add 1 can diced tomatoes or 2 cups fresh diced tomatoes, salt and pepper to taste. Cook until okra is tender. Corn may also be added to this recipe. Serves 6 to 8.

SWEET POTATO PANCAKES

3 pounds sweet potatoes (about 6)	1 teaspoon allspice
2 to 3 eggs	salt and pepper
3 tablespoon flour	6 to 8 tablespoons butter
1 tablespoon honey	granulated sugar

Peel sweet potatoes, cut in quarters and cook in boiling salted water until tender, about 30 minutes. Drain and grate in food processor. In large bowl, lightly whisk 2 of the eggs. Add flour, honey and sweet potatoes. The texture should be that of cooked oatmeal. If too dry, add additional egg. Season with salt, pepper and allspice. Melt butter in skillet. Drop batter by tablespoons into pan and flatten with back of spoon. Cook until lightly browned, turning once. Dust with granulated sugar before serving. Serves 8 to 10.

CHERRY TOMATOES BAKED IN VODKA

2 pints cherry tomatoes	½ teaspoon Crazy Jane salt
⅓ cup vodka	½ teaspoon freshly ground pepper
1 garlic clove, minced	

Preheat oven to 350 degrees. Place tomatoes in a single layer in shallow noncorrodible baking pan. In small bowl, mix together vodka and garlic. Pour over tomatoes. Season with salt and pepper. Bake tomatoes 5 to 8 minutes until heated through. Serves 10.

BROCCOLI WADDIL

2 cups cooked chopped broccoli	½ teaspoon salt
1 tablespoon flour	½ pint light cream
½ cup mayonnaise	3 beaten eggs
1 tablespoon melted butter	

Combine broccoli, flour, butter, mayonnaise, and salt. Add cream and eggs. Pour into well greased baking dish. Place in a pan of hot water and bake at 370 degrees for 55 minutes, or until a knife inserted in the middle comes out clean. Serves 6 to 8.

HERBED GRITS

3 ounces cream cheese, softened
1 cup shredded Cheddar cheese
1 stick butter
2 teaspoons salt
1 teaspoon pepper

1 tablespoon sweet basil
1 tablespoon fresh garlic, minced
½ cup sun dried tomatoes, diced
  (optional)
quick grits

Prepare 12 servings of grits, according to package. After reducing heat to a simmer, add all ingredients, stirring constantly until it is the desired consistency. Serves 10 to 12.

RANCH POTATOES

15 new potatoes, peeled
1 medium onion, sliced in ⅛ inch
  rings
4 tablespoons butter, melted

1 teaspoon salt
1 teaspoon pepper
½ cup Parmesan cheese

Steam or bake potatoes until done, but still firm. Steam for 15 to 20 minutes, or rub with vegetable oil and bake at 400 degrees for 20 minutes. Cut potatoes in half lengthwise and place in baking dish. Toss with remaining ingredients. Cover and bake at 350 degrees for 30 minutes. Garnish with fresh parsley and paprika. Serves 6 to 8.

MA'S POTATOES WITH WHITE SAUCE

Boil six medium potatoes peeled and cut into large chunks. Salt and pepper to taste.

Sauce: Melt ½ stick butter and add 2 tablespoons plain flour. Add 2 cups milk and cook on medium heat until thick. Pour over potatoes and warm together. ½ cup Cheddar cheese may be added if desired. Serves 6 to 8.

SQUASH PUDDING

2 pounds summer squash
2 tablespoons butter
1 egg, beaten
½ cup medium white sauce

2 tablespoons butter
½ cup buttered bread crumbs
1 teaspoon salt
½ teaspoon white pepper

Steam the squash drain and mash. Add butter, egg, white sauce, salt and pepper. Place in a greased casserole dish and top with buttered bread crumbs and sprinkle with paprika.

Bake in 375 degree oven 25 to 30 minutes or until browned. 6 to 8 servings.

SQUASH CASSEROLE

1 pound yellow or zucchini squash   1 chopped onion

Cook squash and onion in small amount of boiling water until tender. Drain well and mash. Add:

1 teaspoon salt
½ stick butter
1 heaping tablespoon sour cream
1 egg

½ cup canned French fried onion
  rings
½ cup grated Cheddar cheese

Pour into greased baking dish. Bake in 375 degree oven for 30 minutes. Remove and top with ½ roll of crushed Ritz crackers blended with ¼ cup melted butter. Return to oven until browned. Serves 6.

PECAN AND SQUASH CASSEROLE

2 pounds cooked yellow squash,
  drained
1 can cream of mushroom soup,
  undiluted

¼ cup sour cream
¼ cup chopped pecans
pinch nutmeg
salt and pepper to taste

Cook squash until tender, drain and mash. Mix with other ingredients. Pour into greased casserole. Top with buttered cracker crumbs. Bake at 350 degrees for 30 minutes or until bubbly around edges and brown on top.

VEGETARIAN STUFFED SQUASH

3 medium sized squash
½ cup thick white sauce, see index
1 tablespoon grated onion
2 tablespoons green bell pepper,
    chopped

3 eggs, hard boiled, chopped
    (optional)
1 cup Colby cheese, grated
½ teaspoon salt
½ teaspoon black pepper
1 cup buttered bread crumbs

Boil the whole squash about 10 minutes until almost tender. Drain and scoop
out centers. Mash pulp; add white sauce, onion, green pepper, eggs, ½ cup of
bread crumbs, salt, pepper and ½ cup of the cheese. Stuff mixture inside
cavities of squash. Place in buttered baking dish with enough water to cover
bottom of dish. Bake at 375 degrees 25 to 30 minutes. Cool about 15 minutes.
Cut each squash in half length wise. Sprinkle with remaining cheese and
bread crumbs. Bake 5 to 10 minutes until lightly browned. Serves 6.

FRIED YELLOW SQUASH

Slice squash. Add salt and pepper to taste. Dip in buttermilk and roll in
breading mix. Deep fry until brown.

Breading Mix:
1 cup self-rising flour
1 cup pancake mix

1 teaspoon paprika

SQUASH CROQUETTES

2 pounds yellow squash, sliced
1 large onion, grated
1 cup plain bread crumbs
2 eggs, slightly beaten

2 teaspoons salt
1 teaspoon black pepper
1 cup sharp Cheddar cheese,
    grated

Steam squash until tender. Drain well. Mash squash and add all ingredients
and stir together. Add more bread crumbs if needed to shape croquettes. Roll
in white corn meal. Deep fry in vegetable oil until golden brown. Drain well
on paper towel. Serve hot. Serves 6 to 8.

FRIED EGGPLANT

We eat these as fast as Ma can cook them.

Peel and cut eggplant into French fry type strips. Soak in icy, salted water for at least 1 hour. Drain well and toss in white self rising corn meal ,seasoned with salt and pepper or ½ plain flour and ½ pancake mix.

Fry in vegetable oil, 350 degrees temperature or on medium high heat until golden brown and crisp. Drain on paper towels; serve immediately.

STEWED CORN

This is a quick way to get the taste of fresh fried corn. Process ½, 8 ounces, package of frozen whole kernel corn with ½ cup water. Add to remaining package of corn. Place in skillet with 1 heaping tablespoon of corn starch, ½ stick butter, salt and pepper to taste. Cook on low heat, 20 to 30 minutes until thick. Add water as needed. Serves 4 to 6.

CORN FRITTERS

1¾ cups plain flour
3 teaspoons baking powder
½ teaspoon salt
1 egg, slightly beaten

1 cup milk
1 tablespoon vegetable oil
1½ cups corn, drained well

Sift flour and measure. Add baking powder and salt; sift again. Combine egg, milk and oil. Pour into flour mixture and stir gently just until smooth. Gently stir in corn. Drop by tablespoonfuls into deep hot vegetable oil (365 degrees) and fry about 3 minutes until brown on all sides, turning fritters as they float to the surface. Drain on paper towels and serve immediately. Serves about 6. *⅓ cup chopped chives can be added to batter if desired.*

HOLIDAY YAMS

1 16-ounce can sliced cling
  peaches
1 tablespoon cornstarch
⅔ cup brown sugar
1 8-ounce can whole berry
  cranberry sauce

½ teaspoon cinnamon
2 tablespoons butter
2 pounds steamed sweet potatoes,
  sliced in 1 inch rounds

Drain peaches, reserving juice. Dissolve cornstarch in ¼ cup peach juice. Set aside. Heat remaining peach juice, brown sugar, cranberry sauce, cinnamon and butter in large skillet until butter is melted. Add cornstarch mixture and stir over medium heat until thickened. Add sweet potatoes; cover skillet and cook 10 minutes. Add peaches and toss gently. Cook additional 5 to 10 minutes until heated through. Makes 6 to 8 servings.

BROCCOLI SOUFFLÉ

1 pound broccoli, chopped
1 large onion, diced
10 saltine crackers, processed
¼ cup butter, melted
2 large eggs, separated

1 cup sharp Cheddar cheese,
  grated
½ cup milk
1 teaspoon salt
½ teaspoon black pepper

Steam broccoli and onion until very tender. Drain well. Add cracker crumbs, butter, egg yolks, cheese, milk, salt and pepper to broccoli mixture and stir. Beat egg whites until stiff but not dry. Gently fold into broccoli mixture. Place into a medium sized greased casserole dish. Bake at 350 degrees 30 minutes until golden brown and firm. Serve immediately. Serves 6.

JALAPEÑO GRITS SOUFFLÉ

Shirley has prepared this dish for many of our brunches.
It is a favorite of our customers.

1 cup milk	¾ cup shredded sharp Cheddar
1 cup water	cheese
2 teaspoons salt	¾ cup shredded Monterey Pepper
1 cup uncooked quick grits	Jack cheese
⅓ cup butter	8 egg whites, room temperature
½ teaspoon black pepper	¼ teaspoon cream of tartar
4 large egg yolks	pepper jelly

Combine milk, water and salt in large saucepan. Bring to a rapid boil and gradually stir in grits. Reduce heat and simmer uncovered for 5 minutes until thickened. Stir occasionally. Remove from heat. Add butter and pepper; stir until butter is melted. Add yolks and cheeses, stirring well. Beat egg whites and cream of tartar at high speed until stiff peaks form. Gently fold ⅓ of the egg whites into grits; gently fold in remaining egg whites.

Pour into greased 9 x 13 inch baking dish. Spread evenly. Bake on center rack of oven at 425 degrees for 30 to 35 minutes until puffed and golden brown. Cut in squares and top with pepper jelly. Serve immediately! Serves 10 to 12. *If desired, bake in a lightly buttered 2-quart soufflé dish. Circle dish with aluminum foil allowing 3 inches above the rim. Butter one side of foil; buttered side against dish. Secure foil with string. Fold foil into thirds for a sturdier collar.*

MAMA'S HOMEMADE PEPPER JELLY

25 hot peppers, or ¼ cup hot	3 cups white vinegar
pepper mixed with 1 cup bell	green or red food coloring
pepper	⅓ cup water
5 pounds sugar	

Mix chopped peppers, water, sugar, vinegar and food coloring. Boil 5 minutes. Remove from heat. Add 2 packages (4 pouches) of Certo. Skim before putting into jars. Seal. Makes 12 8-ounce jars.

GREEN RICE RING

2 cups cooked rice
2 cups grated sharp Cheddar
　　cheese
1 large can evaporated milk
½ cup chopped parsley or
　　2 tablespoons parsley flakes

½ cup chopped green onions
1 stick butter or margarine
4 eggs
1 teaspoon salt
2 large cloves garlic, minced

Sauté onions, minced garlic, and parsley in butter. Beat eggs, add milk and all other ingredients. Bake in a greased and floured ring mold at 350 degrees 30 to 45 minutes. Do not over brown. Unmold and fill with green peas. Beautiful presentation.

FRESH TURNIP GREENS

1 large bunch turnip greens
bacon fat
oleo

salt
1 teaspoon sugar

Strip leaves from stems of greens. Wash 4 times. Place in pot with enough water to cover. Add bacon fat and oleo, salt, and sugar. Cook until tender, about 1 hour. You may wish to substitute fresh pork, bacon or ham (veggie oil is OK, but be sure to add margarine also for flavor).

CREAMED SPINACH IN PASTRY SHELLS

15-20 small pastry shells, baked
2 packages frozen chopped
　　spinach, cooked and squeezed
　　dry as possible

2 cans cream of chicken soup
a little grated onion
dash of cinnamon
2 tablespoons flour

To hot, cooked spinach, add soup, onion and cinnamon. Carefully blend in flour. When well mixed, pour spinach mixture into warm pastry shells. Top with hard boiled eggs which have been grated. Serve around any cold meat or veggie platter.

POTATO CAKE PATTIES

Barbara's mother, Ma, has been making these all her life.
Great way to use left-over mashed potatoes.

4 medium potatoes, cooked and
    mashed
1 small onion, grated
½ cup plain flour

1 egg, slightly beaten
2 teaspoons salt
1 teaspoon pepper

Mix together all ingredients. Heat small amount of oil on medium high heat in skillet. Drop by tablespoon into skillet. Mash down like pancake with back of spoon. Turn once after several minutes until lightly browned. Drain on paper towel. Serve hot. Top with sour cream and sprinkle with chives if desired. Serves 8.

SPINACH TIMBALES

1 pound spinach, washed and
    stems discarded
3 tablespoons butter
2 tablespoons flour
¾ cup milk
½ cup heavy cream

1 teaspoon Crazy Jane salt and
    pepper, to taste
⅛ teaspoon freshly grated nutmeg
1 teaspoon chopped garlic
3 large eggs, beaten

In large saucepan, wilt spinach covered over high heat 4 or 5 minutes. Drain well, squeeze and chop. In a saucepan, melt butter over low heat, whisk in flour and cook for 3 minutes. Remove pan from heat, whisk in milk and cream and bring to boil. Remove from heat and stir in salt, pepper, nutmeg, garlic and spinach. Let cool. Stir in eggs and combine well. Divide among 8 buttered ramekins. Bake in water bath in preheated 375 degree oven for 20 minutes. Remove from water and let cool 5 minutes. Run a knife around the edges, unmold and serve. Yield 8 servings.

Some wild life at Rose Hill. Butterfly enjoys nectar from many blooming plants.

$\mathcal{B}$reads

The Easter Bluebird has her favorite house!

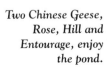

Two Chinese Geese, Rose, Hill and Entourage, enjoy the pond.

PUMPKIN GINGERBREAD MUFFINS

1½ cups plain flour
½ teaspoon salt
½ teaspoon baking soda
2 teaspoons baking powder
¾ teaspoon ground ginger
⅛ teaspoon ground cloves
½ teaspoon ground cinnamon
6 tablespoons butter, softened

⅓ cup brown sugar
⅓ cup sugar
1 egg
½ cup pumpkin purée
½ cup milk
1 cup raisins (optional)
1 cup chopped pecans
sugar and cinnamon mixture

In a bowl sift together flour, salt, baking soda, baking powder, ginger, cloves and cinnamon. Set aside. In large mixing bowl, cream butter with 2 sugars until light and fluffy. Beat in egg and pumpkin purée. Using slow speed of mixer, add dry ingredients and milk to pumpkin mixture, alternating in two batches. Beat well until thoroughly mixed. Stir in raisins and pecans. Fill buttered muffin cups and sprinkle with sugar/cinnamon mixture. Bake in preheated 350 degree oven 25 to 30 minutes. Yield 12 muffins.

ROSE HILL CORNBREAD MUFFINS

Everybody that visits Rose Hill raves about Shirley's cornbread muffins.
They're crisp on the outside and tender on the inside.

1½ cups self rising white corn
   meal (Not corn meal mix!)
½ cup self rising flour

⅓ cup vegetable oil
1 cup buttermilk
2 eggs

Slightly beat eggs with wire whip. Add buttermilk and oil and mix together. Stir in dry ingredients until moistened. Do not stir until smooth. Batter will be slightly lumpy. Spoon into greased muffin tins and bake at 400 degrees 20 to 30 minutes until brown. Serve immediately. Makes 8 to 10 muffins.
Old Fashioned Method: Put ⅓ cup vegetable oil in 10 inch iron skillet. Put into preheated oven for about 10 minutes until oil is hot. Pour batter into skillet and bake for 20 to 30 minutes until brown. Cut into wedges. Serve immediately.

CORN AND JALAPEÑO JELLY MUFFINS

1 cup all-purpose flour
1 cup white cornmeal
1 tablespoon baking powder
¼ cup sugar
1 teaspoon red pepper flakes
2 eggs
½ cup plus 1 tablespoon milk

¼ cup oil
1 10-ounce package frozen corn
  kernels, defrosted
¼ cup jalapeño jelly (We use
  Mama's hot pepper jelly — red
  or green)

Preheat oven to 375 degrees. Spray muffin cup with veggie spray. Mix together flour, cornmeal, sugar, baking powder and pepper flakes. In another bowl, whisk together eggs, milk, oil and corn. Pour liquids over dry ingredients and stir lightly. DO NOT OVER BLEND. Batter will be stiff. Fill each muffin cup about ½ full. Make a small depression in center of each muffin with back of spoon and drop in 1 teaspoon jelly. Divide reserved batter over tops to cover jelly. DO NOT SPREAD. Bake in 375 degree oven 20 to 25 minutes till golden. Let muffins rest in pan about 2 to 5 minutes. Using a blunt knife, ease muffins out onto wire rack. Yields 12 muffins.

GINGERBREAD MUFFINS

1 cup butter, melted
2 cups sugar
4 tablespoons molasses
2 teaspoons ground ginger
2 teaspoons ground cinnamon
1 teaspoon ground cloves

1 teaspoon ground nutmeg
pinch of salt
2 cups buttermilk
2 teaspoons baking soda
2 eggs, well beaten
3 cups plain flour

To melted butter, stir in next 7 ingredients. Dissolve soda in buttermilk, and add to butter, spice mixture. Stir in vanilla and beaten eggs. Add flour last. Fill greased and floured muffin tins. Bake at 350 degrees until toothpick comes out clean. Approximately 12 muffins.

KATIE'S SWEDISH PANCAKES

Shirley's niece, Katie, learned how to make these pancakes in her Home Economics Class in Huntsville. They are delicious. Her brother Michael said he could eat a hundred of them.

3 eggs
¾ cup sifted plain flour
1 tablespoon sugar

1¼ cups milk
½ teaspoon salt

Filling:
½ cup cream cheese, room
   temperature
¼ cup sour cream

¼ teaspoon grated lemon zest
¼ teaspoon vanilla extract

Beat eggs until thick and lemon colored. Stir in milk. Sift dry ingredients and add to egg mixture, mixing until smooth. Drop by tablespoon onto moderately hot buttered griddle. Spread batter evenly to make thin cakes. Turn once when underside is light brown. Sprinkle with sugar and stack.

Filling: Mix all ingredients together. Place about 1 tablespoon of the filling on one end of pancake and roll up. Top each with strawberry preserves that have been warmed with a little butter.

SPOON BREAD

1 cup self-rising white cornmeal
½ cup self rising flour

1 egg
1½ cups buttermilk

Sift meal and flour into bowl. Make well in center. Whisk egg and buttermilk together. Pour into well. Stir just until moistened. Drop by heaping tablespoons into small amount of preheated oil in skillet. Fry on medium high heat until brown, turning once. Drain on paper towel. Serve hot. Makes approximately 10 to 12.

CINNAMON SUGAR MUFFINS

This muffin recipe was developed by Barbara's mother, Ma, for her daddy, who was unable to eat cornbread. This was a smoother texture he could tolerate.

2 cups self rising flour
¼ cup sugar
2 eggs

⅓ cup vegetable oil
1¼ cups buttermilk
cinnamon/sugar (mix to taste)

Beat eggs, oil and buttermilk with wire whip just until mixed. Do not over beat. Add flour and sugar and stir until dry ingredients are moistened. Do not over stir; batter should be slightly lumpy. Spoon into greased muffin tins and top with cinnamon sugar. Bake at 350 degrees for 25 to 30 minutes. Makes 10 to 12 muffins.

Cheese Muffins: Omit sugar and stir 1 cup shredded Cheddar cheese into flour before stirring with buttermilk mixture.

Blueberry Muffins: Prepare as for cinnamon sugar muffins. Toss 1 cup well-drained berries into flour before stirring with buttermilk mixture. Stir gently so you don't mash blueberries. Glaze: 1 cup powdered sugar, ¼ cup milk, 2 teaspoons melted butter, 1 teaspoon vanilla. Brush glaze over hot blueberry muffins. More or less milk can be used to reach desired consistency of glaze.

QUINCY'S NO RISE ROLLS

1 package yeast
2 cups warm water
¼ cup sugar

1 egg
1½ sticks butter, melted
4 cups self-rising flour

Soften yeast in warm water. Using electric mixer, mix all ingredients together well. Fill greased muffin tins ⅔ full. Bake in preheated 400 degree oven 20 to 30 minutes until golden brown. Brush additional melted butter over tops. So easy and so good. Leftover batter keeps well in covered container for 2 weeks. Allow room in container for rising. Approximately 2 dozen rolls.

MA'S YEAST ROLLS

We have served these rolls many times at Panache at Rose Hill with Shirley's wonderful tenderloin, which is always a favorite for cocktail buffets. Ma has shared hundreds of these with the residents at her retirement home, SETON HAVEN.

Heat 1 cup milk and add 1 stick margarine, ¼ cup sugar and 2 teaspoons salt. Set aside to cool. Dissolve 1 package yeast in ½ cup warm water and 1 tablespoon sugar. Let proof and add yeast mixture to milk mixture and blend in enough plain flour to make a stiff dough. Knead until elastic. Put into greased bowl, cover, and place in warm place until dough doubles in bulk. Roll out on floured board, cut into shapes and place on greased baking sheet. Bake at 400 degrees until brown. Brush with melted butter. Makes 30 large or 60 small rolls.

MARTHA'S WHOLE WHEAT ROLLS

1 cup shortening
1 cup boiling water
½ cup sugar
1 cup All Bran
6 cups plain flour

1½ teaspoons salt
2 packages yeast
1 cup lukewarm water
2 eggs, beaten

Combine shortening, boiling water, sugar, bran and salt. Stir until shortening melts. Cool and add yeast dissolved in warm water. Add beaten eggs and 2 cups of the flour and beat until light. Add rest of flour and place in covered bowl. At this point, you may refrigerate until ready to use, or roll out and cut into desired shape and place on greased baking sheets. Let rise until double in size. Bake at 400 degrees until brown. Approximately 5 to 6 dozen rolls.

SOUR CREAM BISCUITS

1 cup butter, melted   2 cups self-rising flour
1 cup sour cream

Combine butter and sour cream. Blend in flour, mixing thoroughly. Fill ungreased mini-muffin pans with heaping teaspoons batter. Bake at 400 degrees 15 minutes. Cool slightly before removing from pans. Makes 30 mini-biscuits.

OLD FASHION BUTTERMILK BISCUITS

2 cups self rising flour   1 cup buttermilk
5 tablespoons plus 1 teaspoon
    chilled shortening

Cut shortening into flour until it resembles coarse meal. Make well in center of flour mixture. Pour buttermilk in well and stir with hand until all flour is incorporated. Additional tablespoons of buttermilk may be added if mixture seems too dry. Dough will be tacky. Sprinkle 1 to 2 cups flour on counter. Place dough onto floured surface. Sprinkle flour over dough and hands. Knead, rolling sides inward to center of dough with hands very gently about 10 times. Again, knead very gently! Lightly pat out to about an 8 inch round and then roll with rolling pin using a light touch. Roll out to ½ to ¾ inch thickness , depending on desired size of biscuit. Cut out biscuits with 3 inch cutter and place on well greased baking sheet. Leave no space between biscuits. Brush tops with melted butter and bake at 450 degrees for 15 to 20 minutes or until golden brown. Makes 10 to 15 biscuits depending on thickness of dough before cutting.

BLUEBERRY BUTTERMILK BISCUITS

2 cups all-purpose flour
1 tablespoon baking powder
¼ teaspoon baking soda
1 teaspoon salt
½ cup sugar

1 teaspoon grated orange rind
⅓ cup shortening
1 egg, beaten
¾ cup buttermilk
½ cup blueberries

Glaze:
3 tablespoons melted butter
3 tablespoons sugar

¼ teaspoon cinnamon
⅛ teaspoon nutmeg

Combine first 6 ingredients, cut in shortening. Combine egg and buttermilk; add to flour mixture. Stir till moistened. Stir in blueberries. Turn onto floured surface. Knead 4 or 5 times. Roll dough to ½ inch thickness. Cut with biscuit cutter. Place on greased baking sheets. Bake at 400 degrees for 15 minutes. Combine remaining ingredients. Brush on warm biscuits. Yield 15 biscuits.

BLACK-EYED PEA CORNBREAD

1 cup canned black-eyed peas,
    drained
1 cup white cornmeal
½ cup flour
1 teaspoon salt
½ teaspoon baking soda
2 eggs
1 cup buttermilk

½ cup corn oil
1½ cups grated Cheddar cheese
1 chopped onion
¾ cup cream style corn
½ cup chopped red and green bell
    pepper
1 pound ground beef, browned,
    drained and crumbled

Mix all ingredients and pour into 8 x 8 inch greased baking pan and bake at 350 degrees for 45 minutes. Serves 6 to 8.

MA'S DRESSING

Crumble one 9 x 9 pan cooked cornbread (your favorite cornbread recipe).
Tear 8 slices bread into pieces.
Set aside
Heat 2 quarts water with 8 chicken bouillon cubes
Add 3 cups chopped onions and 3 cups chopped celery
Add drippings from baked chicken or turkey
Add pepper to taste

Cook until tender. Pour over bread mixture and mash up. When cool, add 4
eggs. Don't make mixture too stiff. Add water or milk as needed. Bake at 400
degrees until brown. Serves 8 to 10.

PIZZA CORN BREAD

2 cups self-rising cornmeal
¼ cup liquid vegetable oil
2 eggs
1 cup buttermilk
¼ cup chopped green pepper
1 teaspoon chopped hot pepper
1 teaspoon ground black pepper
½ cup chopped pepperoni
1 teaspoon dried oregano
1 small onion, chopped
1 cup grated cheese

Combine cornmeal, milk, eggs and oil until blended. Add remaining ingredients. Pour batter into greased black skillet or pan. Cook in preheated 400
degree oven for 20 minutes or until browned. Serves 8 to 10.

DABBO'S CORNBREAD DRESSING

6 slices white bread
6 cups cornbread, crumbled (see
   cornbread recipe in index)
1 cup celery, chopped
1 large onion, chopped
4 cups chicken broth

2 tablespoons prepared mustard
3 tablespoons melted butter
¼ teaspoon sage
1 teaspoon poultry seasoning
salt and pepper to taste
pinch of sugar

Put bread on baking sheet and toast in 200 degree oven until bread is golden brown and crisp like melba toast. Cook onion and celery in small amount of broth to cover. Simmer until tender. Pour over broken toast and let cool. Mash with hands until there are no lumps of toast. Combine all other ingredients and mix well. Pour into greased 13 x 9 inch casserole dish. Brush top of dressing with drippings from turkey or additional butter. Bake at 350 degrees for approximately 30 minutes or until lightly brown on top. Serves 10 to 12.

Giblet Gravy: Cook turkey neck, liver and gizzards from turkey, covering with water. Cook until meat from neck pulls off bone easily. Reserve liquid and add additional chicken broth to make 2 cups. Brown 4 tablespoons plain flour on low heat in skillet, stirring frequently until brown. Be careful for it will burn easily. Melt 3 tablespoons butter in small sauce pan and stir flour in and add broth mixture slowly with wire whip, cooking on medium heat until thickened. Add diced liver, gizzards, meat from neck and grated egg.

MA'S HUSH PUPPIES

2 cups corn meal
1 cup flour
2 tablespoons sugar
½ teaspoon baking soda

2 eggs
1 small grated onion
buttermilk (about 1 cup)

Blend wet ingredients, then add dry. Batter should be consistency of thick cake batter. Drop by teaspoons into hot oil. Turn once when brown. Drain on brown paper bags. Serves 6 to 8.

BREADING FOR FRIED FISH

We eat a lot fish in the South; especially catfish. This breading makes a beautiful golden crust. Just don't overcook the fish. We fry our fish in peanut oil or vegetable oil.

1½ cups self-rising cornmeal
1½ cups pancake mix

1 tablespoon paprika
1 tablespoon pepper

Mix ingredients together. Use to dip fish in before frying.

Bob and John enjoy the horses. There are now eleven horses, and three more on the way!

$\mathcal{D}$esserts

Goldie herds her three chicks, Winkin, Blinkin and Nod, into the compost bin.

Country living at its finest! Precious and Precious, II enjoy a leisurely afternoon.

BLUEBERRY PIE

1 cup sugar
4 to 6 tablespoons flour
   (depending on juiciness of
   berries)
¼ teaspoon salt

5 cups fresh blueberries, washed
   and drained
1 tablespoon fresh lemon juice
3 tablespoons butter
2 9-inch pie shells

Prepare Standard Pastry, see index. Combine sugar, flour and salt. Sprinkle ½ of sugar mixture over bottom of chilled, unbaked pastry shell in 9 inch pie pan. Add blueberries and sprinkle with remaining sugar mixture. Drizzle lemon juice over top and dot with butter. Cover with top crust, sealing edges well. Bake on lower shelf of 425 degree oven for 30 to 40 minutes until golden brown. Cool and serve with vanilla ice cream or whipped cream. For a glossy finish, brush top pastry with slightly beaten egg whites being careful not to puddle. Sprinkle lightly with sugar.

KEY LIME PIE

1½ envelopes unflavored gelatin
¾ cup sugar
¼ teaspoon salt
4 egg yolks
2 teaspoons lime zest
⅔ cup fresh lime juice
¼ cup water

2 drops green food coloring
   (optional)
4 egg whites
¾ cup sugar
2 cups whipping cream
1 teaspoon vanilla extract
1 9-inch pie shell, baked

Combine gelatin, ¾ cup sugar and salt in saucepan. Beat egg yolks, lime juice, and water until blended and stir into gelatin. Cook over medium heat until mixture begins to boil. Remove from heat and add lime zest. Add food coloring to give a pale green color; stir well. Chill until mixture thickens, stirring occasionally. Should be consistency of a soft pudding. Beat egg whites until soft peaks form. Gradually add ½ cup sugar and beat until stiff peaks form. Fold into chilled gelatin mixture. Whip 1 cup of cream until soft peaks form and fold into gelatin, egg white mixture. Mound in baked pastry shell, cooled. Chill until firm. Whip remaining cup of whipping cream until soft peaks form, add ¼ cup sugar and 1 teaspoon vanilla extract and continue beating for several minutes until peaks hold shape. Spread on pie and garnish with thin lime twist.

SOUTHERN PECAN PIE

1 stick butter
1 cup light Karo syrup
1 cup sugar
3 large eggs, beaten
1½ teaspoons vanilla extract

¼ teaspoon salt
1 cup chopped pecans
1 9-inch unbaked pie shell (see index)

Brown butter in saucepan on medium low heat until golden brown. Watch carefully, butter will burn quickly. Let cool. Mix all other ingredients well. Blend in browned butter. Pour into unbaked pie shell and bake at 425 degrees for 10 minutes. Lower temperature to 325 degrees and bake for 40 minutes.

BUTTERMILK PIE
WITH BLACKBERRY SAUCE

This is a Rose Hill favorite!

3 large eggs
1 cup sugar
2 tablespoons plain flour
1 stick melted butter, slightly cooled

1 cup buttermilk
2 teaspoons real vanilla extract
1 unbaked 9-inch pie shell (see index)

Sauce:
½ cup seedless blackberry preserves

1 tablespoon Chamborde liqueur

Beat eggs slightly. Mix sugar and flour well and add to eggs. Mix until creamy. Add melted butter mixing well. Add buttermilk and flavoring . Bake at 325 degrees for 45 minutes to 1 hour until custard is set.

Sauce: Put preserves in saucepan and warm on medium heat, stirring constantly with wire whip until smooth. Remove from heat and add Chamborde. Let cool to lukewarm and serve over warm pie.

EGG CUSTARD PIE

1 cup sugar
2 tablespoons plain flour
¼ teaspoon salt
3 eggs, well beaten
3 tablespoons butter, melted

1½ cups milk, room temperature
1 teaspoon vanilla extract
1 9-inch unbaked pastry shell (see index)

Combine sugar, flour and salt. Beat eggs until lemon in color and blend in dry ingredients. Add melted butter and milk. Mix well. Pour into 9-inch pastry shell and bake at 375 degrees for 30 minutes. Allow to set before serving.

SWEET POTATO PIE

1½ cups mashed cooked fresh sweet potatoes
1 stick butter, melted
1½ cups sugar
3 tablespoons plain flour
2 eggs

⅔ cup evaporated milk (do not substitute)
1 teaspoon vanilla extract
½ teaspoon cinnamon
1 9-inch unbaked pie shell (see index)

Mix sugar and flour well with hand. Add all ingredients, beating until smooth and pour into a 9-inch unbaked pie shell. Bake at 375 degrees for about 45 minutes until knife comes out clean when inserted in center. Serve with Pouring Custard.

POURING CUSTARD

2½ cups milk
2 teaspoons vanilla extract

8 large egg yolks
½ cup sugar

Scald milk in heavy medium saucepan. Remove from heat, cover and let stand 20 minutes. Using mixer, beat yolks and sugar in medium bowl until pale yellow. Strain milk. Gradually beat into egg mixture. Return mixture to saucepan and stir over low heat until custard thickens and coats back of spoon, about 15 minutes; do not boil. Strain into bowl, add vanilla. Refrigerate until cool, stirring occasionally. Custard will be thin. Makes about 2½ cups. Pour 3 to 4 tablespoons onto plate. Place slice of sweet potato pie on top of custard. Top pie with whipped cream and cinnamon stick.

FUDGE PIE

2 eggs
1 cup sugar
½ cup butter, melted
½ cup unsifted plain flour

⅓ cup cocoa
¼ teaspoon salt
1 tablespoon vanilla extract
½ cup chopped walnuts

Fudge Sauce:
¾ cup sugar
½ cup cocoa
⅔ cup evaporated milk (do not substitute)

⅓ cup light corn syrup
⅓ cup butter
1 tablespoon Kahlúa or Grand Marnier

Beat sugar and melted butter for about 5 minutes. Add eggs and blend well. Sift flour, cocoa and salt together and add to butter, egg mixture. Blend just until dry ingredients are moistened. Stir in vanilla and nuts. Pour into lightly buttered 8-inch pie plate. Bake at 350 degrees for 25 to 30 minutes or until almost set (pie will not test done). Cool and cut into wedges topped with whipped cream or ice cream and Hot Fudge Sauce.

Fudge Sauce: Combine sugar and cocoa in small saucepan. Blend in evaporated milk and corn syrup. Cook over medium heat, stirring constantly, until mixture boils. Boil and stir for 1 minute; no longer. Remove from heat and stir in butter and liqueur. Let cool for about 30 minutes before topping ice cream.

DANIELLE AND KATIE'S FAVORITE CHOCOLATE CHIP PIE

½ cup butter, softened
2 eggs, beaten
2 tablespoons vanilla extract or bourbon
1 cup sugar

½ cup plain flour
1 cup semi-sweet chocolate chips
1 cup walnuts, chopped
1 9-inch unbaked pie shell (see index)

Beat butter and sugar with mixer until creamy. Add eggs, vanilla and flour and beat well. Stir in chocolate chips and walnuts. Pour into unbaked pastry shell and bake at 350 degrees for 50 minutes or until golden brown. Cool about 45 minutes and serve warm with vanilla ice cream.

LEMON CLOUD PIE

Crust:

2 sticks butter, softened
2 cups plain flour
6 tablespoons sugar

½ cup pecans, finely chopped
1 teaspoon vanilla extract

Filling:

1½ cups sugar
8 tablespoons cornstarch
¼ teaspoon salt
2 cups water

3 egg yolks
2 tablespoons butter
2 teaspoons lemon zest
½ cup fresh lemon juice

Beat sugar and butter until creamy. Add remaining ingredients and mix well. Press dough into bottom of an 8 x 8 inch baking pan. Bake at 325 degrees about 20 to 30 minutes until golden brown. Crust will crisp up as it cools. Always, if using glass pans, reduce oven temperature 25 degrees.

Filling: Combine sugar, cornstarch and salt in top of double boiler. Stir in water and cook over boiling water until thickened, stirring constantly. Cover and cook 15 minutes longer. Stir a little of the hot mixture into slightly beaten egg yolks; add to remaining hot mixture in top of double boiler and cook for 2 minutes, stirring constantly. Add butter and cool. Add lemon zest and lemon juice, stir well. Pour mixture into cooled pie crust and chill. Top with whipped cream.

ANGEL NUT PIE

3 egg whites
½ teaspoons baking powder
1 cup chopped pecans

1 cup sugar
20 Ritz crackers
1 teaspoon vanilla

Chocolate Sauce:
1 cup sugar
¼ cup cocoa

½ cup evaporated milk
1 teaspoon vanilla

Beat egg whites until stiff. Add sugar and baking powder. Crunch crackers and add to above mixture. Add nuts and vanilla. Pour into well greased 9-inch pie plate and bake 30 minutes at 350 degrees. Let cool and cut into wedges. Top with whipped cream and chocolate sauce.

Chocolate Sauce: Mix and boil about 5 minutes. Let cool.

LEMON CHESS PIE

*This is my favorite chess pie from a recipe shared by
our friend Sally Griffin, who served as decorator, confidant, gardner
and general flunky.*

2 cups sugar
1 tablespoon flour
1 tablespoon cornmeal
4 eggs
¼ cup butter, melted

¼ cup milk
4 tablespoons grated lemon rind
¼ cup lemon juice
1 unbaked 9 inch pastry shell

Combine sugar, flour and cornmeal. Toss lightly with fork. Add eggs, butter, milk, lemon rind and juice. Beat until smooth. Pour into pastry shell. Bake at 375 degrees 35 to 45 minutes.

JAPANESE FRUIT PIE

This is another of Mose's recipes.

4 eggs
1 cup coconut
1 cup chopped pecans
1 cup raisins
2 sticks melted butter

2 cups sugar
½ teaspoon apple cider vinegar
2 teaspoons vanilla
2 9-inch pie shells

Beat eggs slightly and add other ingredients. Pour into pie shells and bake at 300 degrees for 50 to 55 minutes. Makes 2 (9 inch) pies.

MA'S FRIED PIES

Bob, Barbara's husband, loves these. He sprinkles powdered sugar over his.

Blend together:
1½ cups self rising flour
1½ cups plain flour

1 teaspoon salt

Cut in ⅓ cup shortening. Add enough buttermilk to make stiff dough. Roll out on floured surface. Cut circles using small coffee saucer as pattern. Drop a tablespoon of sweetened stewed fruit on circle. Fold over moistened edges and seal by mashing with tines of fork. Prick top several times. Fry in ¼ to ½ inch vegetable oil in skillet on medium high heat turning once until golden brown on each side. Drain well on paper towels.

STANDARD PIE PASTRY

2 cups plain flour
1 teaspoon salt

⅔ cup shortening, chilled
6 to 8 tablespoons ice water

Sift flour, measure, add salt and sift again. Cut half of the shortening in with pastry cutter or hand until mixture resembles coarse meal. Cut remaining shortening in until second half of shortening resembles small peas. Move flour mixture to one side of bowl. Put 1 tablespoon of water at a time on opposite side of bowl. With fork, incorporate small amounts of flour (about ¼ cup) into water just until flour particles are absorbed; pressing lightly with fork. Do not stir. Repeat until all of the flour has been absorbed. Dough should not be tacky. Divide dough into 2 pieces and press into balls very gently with hands; wrap and chill for 30 to 40 minutes before rolling out. Remember, the less the dough is handled, the flakier the pastry will be. Remove from refrigerator to well floured surface. Allow dough to sit for 10 minutes. With hands, gently press dough out into a 5 to 6 inch circle. Roll dough out at this point with rolling pin to a 10½ inch circle, turning frequently to make sure surface is still well floured beneath. While rolling, if dough tears on edges, just lightly press together with fingers. Carefully roll pastry around rolling pin and unroll into pie plate. Chill before filling. Fill with desired mixture and repeat steps for top crust. Moisten edges of bottom crust with water and place top crust over pie. Trim edges with knife or pastry scissors ¼ inch wider than pie plate. Tuck under and press with floured tines of fork or flute. Most pies bake at 425 degrees for 30 to 40 minutes on lower shelf in oven unless recipe states otherwise. Makes two 9 inch pie crust or one two-crust pie.

Baked Pastry Shell:

After placing pastry in pie plate, prick the pastry well with fork, sides and bottom. Chill then bake on upper shelf of 450 degree oven 10 to 15 minutes until lightly browned. Transfer to lower shelf after crust is set, if the edges are browning too fast. Cool shell before filling.

Rich, Buttery Pastry:

Roll entire dough of Standard Pie Pastry into oblong shape ⅛ inch thick. Dot with 2½ tablespoons butter. Roll up jelly roll fashion. Roll out again into oblong shape and fold in sides to make 3 layers. Fold in ends the same way,

(Continued on page 127)

(Continued from page 126)

making 9 layers. Wrap and chill and proceed as for standard recipe. Using this method , by rolling twice, and folding over before chilling, creates swirls of butter throughout pastry. Also wonderful used for tarts, turnovers and other small pastries.

MA'S PIE CRUST

2 cups plain flour
¾ cup Crisco

1 teaspoon salt
ice water to make stiff dough

Cut Crisco into flour blended with salt. Add enough water to make stiff dough. Roll out on floured countertop and place in pie plate. Makes 2 pie crusts.

AUNT DOT'S BLACKBERRY COBBLER

1½ cups sugar
2 cups water
½ cup butter
½ cup shortening

1½ cups self rising flour
⅓ cup milk
3 cups blackberries
1 teaspoon lemon juice

Cook sugar and water in a saucepan over medium heat, stirring constantly until sugar is dissolved. Set aside. Place butter in a 13 x 9 x 2 inch baking dish in a 350 degree oven until butter melts (about 3 minutes). Set aside. Cut shortening into flour until mixture resembles coarse meal; add milk stirring just until dry ingredients are moistened. Knead 4 or 5 times on lightly floured surface. Roll into 12 x 9 inch rectangle. Spread blackberries , tossed in lemon juice over dough. Roll up jelly roll fashion. Cut dough into 12 - 1 inch slices. Place slices cut side down in butter. Pour sugar syrup around slices. Bake at 350 degrees 55 to 60 minutes or until golden brown.

DABBO'S APPLE PAN DOWDY

Pastry:

1½ cups plain flour

dash of salt

½ cup shortening

ice water

Filling:

½ cup sugar

½ teaspoon cinnamon

¼ teaspoon salt

¼ teaspoon nutmeg

¼ cup water

10 large Granny Smith Apples, peeled, cored and sliced into thin wedges

½ cup maple syrup

3 tablespoons melted butter

Sift flour and salt together. Add shortening, mixing until crumbly. Add just enough ice water to hold mixture together. Next, roll out dough. Brush dough with melted butter and cut it in half. Fold over and cut into quarters. Fold once more and cut these last pieces in two. Each time, brush the pieces with butter. The net of all of this cutting is a lot of small pieces of pastry which are piled on top of one another. Chill 1 hour before rolling. Divide pastry in half and roll out bottom crust and line a 13 x 9 x 2 inch dish.

Filling: Mix sugar, cinnamon, salt and nutmeg. Put apples in pastry lined baking dish. Sprinkle sugar mixture over apples and lightly toss. Mix maple syrup with butter and water and pour over apples. Now, add the top crust and bake for 10 minutes at 400 degrees; reduce heat to 325 degrees. At this point, dowdy the dessert by cutting the top crust into the apples using a butcher knife and spoon; chopping pastry so ends stick up. Put dessert back in oven and bake for 1 hour at the lower heat. Serve hot with vanilla ice cream. Serves 8 to 10. This dessert is a little time consuming but well worth the trouble. Dabbo has made this since I was a child, and if we were lucky, Mikey didn't eat it all!

PIONEER PEACH COBBLER

This is a favorite at our Easter brunch.

1 stick butter
1 cup sugar
1 cup self rising flour

1 cup milk
1½ cups canned peaches in heavy
    syrup, drained (reserve juice)
¼ cup brown sugar

Melt butter and pour in a 1 quart casserole dish. Mix flour, sugar and milk together and pour over butter in dish. Do not stir! Place peaches on top of batter and pour reserved juice over fruit. Sprinkle with brown sugar and bake at 350 degrees for 1 hour. Top with ice cream. Serves 6.

OLD FASHIONED STRAWBERRY SHORTCAKE

4 cups plain flour
1 teaspoon salt
¼ cup sugar
2 tablespoons baking powder
1 cup butter
2 beaten eggs

1⅓ cups Half & Half
2 cups whipping cream
½ cup sugar
2 teaspoons vanilla extract
4 cups fresh sliced strawberries
¾ cup sugar

Toss ¾ cup sugar over strawberries and toss. Lightly mash berries, being careful not to bruise too much and stir again. Set aside. Stir together dry ingredients. Cut in butter to form coarse crumb mixture. Mix eggs and Half & Half; stir into dry ingredients. Spread into two greased 8-inch spring form cake pans, pressing up side of pan ½ inch. Bake at 450 degrees about 15 to 20 minutes. Cool 10 minutes; remove from pans and cool. Whip cream until soft peaks form, add sugar gradually and vanilla , continue to beat until peaks hold there shapes. Place one shortcake round, ridge up, on platter. Drain strawberries and drizzle half of juice over top of shortcake. Spread half of the strawberries then half of the whip cream on top of cake. Stack with second short cake, ridge side up and repeat steps. Garnish with whole strawberries. Serve immediately. Fresh peaches are also delicious. Serves 8.

LANE CAKE

This cake is a specialty Christmas cake. Shirley's mother, Dabbo, has made this for many years. She prefers to use Bourbon. It is truly a southern tradition.

8 egg whites, beaten
1 cup butter
2 cups sugar
1 cup sweet milk

3 cups flour
2 teaspoons baking powder
1 teaspoon vanilla

Cream butter and sugar until perfectly light. Add milk alternately with flour and baking powder. Fold in egg whites. Pour into three 8 inch or four 6 inch cake pans that have been greased and floured. Bake at 375 degrees for 25 to 30 minutes until lightly browned.

Filling:
8 egg yolks
1 cup sugar
1 box seedless raisins (chopped or ground)
1 cup coconut or 1 coconut

½ cup butter
1 pound pecans (chopped fine)
1 teaspoon vanilla
½ cup wine or bourbon

Beat egg yolks slightly. Add sugar and butter. Cook in double boiler until thick, stirring constantly. Add all other ingredients and cook 5 minutes longer. Spread thick between layers and on top and sides of cake.

BARBARA'S FAVORITE CHEESECAKE

This is Barbara's son, Bill McCorvey, Jr.'s, favorite dessert.

Make graham cracker crust according to package directions and press into pie plate. Bake at 400 degrees for about 10 minutes.

Filling:

Mix 1 pound softened cream cheese, ⅔ cups sugar and 2 well beaten eggs. Pour into crust and bake at 350 degrees for 20 minutes. Remove from oven and top with ½ pint sour cream, 2 teaspoons vanilla and 4 tablespoons sugar mixed together. Bake 15 minutes more.

SHIRLEY'S APPLE WALNUT CAKE

We have many customers who request this cake.

3 eggs
1½ cups vegetable oil
2 cups sugar
3 cups plain flour
1 teaspoon salt
2 teaspoons cinnamon

1 teaspoon baking soda
2 teaspoons vanilla extract
3 cups Granny Smith apples,
    peeled and diced
1½ cups chopped walnuts

Topping:
1 cup brown sugar
¼ cup milk

1 stick butter

Beat eggs, vegetable oil and sugar well. Sift flour, salt, soda and cinnamon together. Add to creamed mixture and mix well on low speed. Add vanilla, apples and walnuts. Pour into greased 9 inch tube pan. Bake at 350 degrees for 1 hour. Remove from oven and pour hot topping over cake in pan.

Topping: Combine all ingredients in saucepan and cook for about 3 minutes until mixture begins to boil. Immediately pour over hot cake in pan. Let cake cool completely in pan before removing.

COCONUT POUND CAKE

6 eggs, separated
½ cup shortening
1 cup butter
3 cups sugar
½ teaspoon almond extract

½ teaspoon coconut extract
3 cups sifted cake flour
1 cup milk
2 cups canned flaked coconut

Bring all ingredients to room temperature. Preheat oven to 300 degrees. Separate eggs. Set egg whites aside. Beat egg yolks with softened shortening and butter until blended. Gradually add sugar, beating until light and fluffy. Add extracts and beat in. At low speed, beat in flour and milk alternately, beginning and ending with flour. Add coconut and beat in on low speed. Beat egg whites until stiff peaks form and gently fold into batter. Pour into greased and floured 10 inch tube pan. Bake for 1 hour and 50 minutes or until toothpick inserted near middle comes out clean. Cool in pan for 10 minutes and remove to wire rack to continue cooling. Put in airtight container for 48 hours before serving.

CHOCOLATE POUND CAKE

½ pound butter
½ cup vegetable shortening
3 cups sugar
5 eggs
3 cups plain flour

2 teaspoons baking powder
½ cup cocoa
½ teaspoon salt
1¼ cups milk
1 tablespoon Kahlúa Liqueur

Glaze:
1 cup powdered sugar
¼ cup milk

1 teaspoon vanilla

Cream butter and shortening. Gradually add sugar. Add eggs one at a time beating well after each. Sift flour, cocoa, baking powder and salt together 3 times to incorporate cocoa well. Add to creamed mixture alternately with milk, beginning and ending with flour. Add Kahlúa. Pour into 10 inch tube pan that has been greased and floured. Batter will be thinner than most pound cakes. Bake at 325 degrees for 1¼ to 1½ hours until toothpick inserted in center comes out clean. Cool for 10 minutes and remove from pan to wire rack to continue cooling. Drizzle thick white glaze over top and garnish with chocolate curls.

COLLEEN'S SOUR CREAM COFFEE CAKE

1 cup butter, softened
1½ cups sugar
2 eggs
1 cup sour cream
2 cups sifted plain flour
½ teaspoon baking soda

1½ teaspoons baking powder
1 teaspoon vanilla extract
¾ cup chopped pecans
2 teaspoons cinnamon
2 tablespoons brown sugar

In large mixing bowl, combine butter, sugar and eggs. Beat until light and fluffy. Blend in sour cream. Resift flour with soda and baking powder. At low speed, add to creamed mixture. Add vanilla, blend well on low speed. Mix nuts with cinnamon and brown sugar. Spoon ⅓ batter into well greased and floured bundt pan (batter will be thick). Sprinkle ⅓ of the nut filling over batter. Spoon ⅓ more batter into pan and sprinkle with nut filling. Repeat with balance of batter ending with nut mixture. Place in cold oven and bake at 350 degrees for 55 minutes.

AUNT JACKIE'S POUND CAKE

Barbara's Aunt Jackie taught her to make this when Barbara was a teenager. She's been making it since.

Cream:
1⅔ cups sugar
1 stick butter

½ cup shortening

Add:
5 eggs one at the time, beating well after each addition

Add alternately with 5 tablespoons milk or orange juice:
2 cups plain flour
½ teaspoon baking powder
½ teaspoon salt

Add:
2 teaspoons vanilla extract or
1 teaspoon vanilla extract and 1 teaspoon orange extract.

Pour into greased and floured tubepan. Bake at 325 degrees for 1 hour and 15 minutes.

FRIED APPLES

2 cups sliced cored apples,
  unpeeled
1 cup sugar
½ cup water

2 tablespoons fresh bacon
  drippings (optional)
dash of salt

Have drippings hot in a heavy skillet (butter or margarine may be substituted for bacon drippings). Add other ingredients, cover and cook until syrup thickens - just a few minutes. Reheats nicely.

BROWNIE ICE CREAM

Another recipe our friend Sally Griffin shared with us.

1 9x12-pan brownies   1 gallon vanilla ice cream

Cook and cool brownies. Remove ice cream from freezer for about 45 minutes. Crumble brownies into ice cream and mix. Return to freezer until ice cream has refrozen. May be served with chocolate sauce.

CHOCOLATE ALMOND MOUSSE

This is also a favorite of Shirley's Dad, Mikey. She could not have been more than 5 or 6 years old when late one night, after everyone was in bed, she ventured up to the kitchen and caught Mikey devouring the remaining half of the pie. It was a romantic setting he had arranged for himself and the pie, with no lights on but the one that shown from the open refrigerator.

18 Jet marshmallows
½ cup milk
6 Hershey almond bars, chopped
2 tablespoons Kahlúa

4 cups heavy whipping cream
  (reserve 1 cup for topping)
1 cup sugar

Melt marshmallows and milk over low heat stirring often, until marshmallows have melted. Remove from heat and stir in chocolate until melted; let cool. Stir in Kahlúa.

Whip 3 cups of cream until it holds soft peaks. Gradually add ¾ cup sugar and beat until stiff peaks form. Fold into chocolate mixture. Put into stemmed glasses, chill. Whip remaining 1 cup of cream until soft peaks form. Gradually add ¼ cup sugar and 1 teaspoon vanilla extract until stiff peaks form. Pipe or spread on top of each mousse. Garnish with stemmed cherry and mint leaf. Serves 8 to 10. This mixture also makes a wonderful pie poured into a 9 inch graham cracker crust and topped with whip cream and chocolate curls.

AUNT NAN'S BROWNIES

2 eggs
1½ cups light brown sugar, packed
⅔ cup vegetable oil (Do Not Use
    Lite Oil)
1 teaspoon vanilla
1½ cups plain flour, sifted

1½ teaspoons baking powder
¾ teaspoon salt
5 ounces semi-sweet chocolate
    chips
½ cup chopped pecans

Beat eggs until foamy and light. Add brown sugar, oil and vanilla and beat well. Sift flour, baking powder and salt together. Stir into creamed mixture. Last, stir in chocolate and pecans. Bake in greased 10 x 15 inch pan in 350 degree oven for 25 minutes. NO LONGER! While still hot, lightly dust with powdered sugar. Cool before cutting.

OLD FASHIONED LIZZIES

1 cup brown sugar
3 well beaten eggs
¾ pound seedless white raisins
3 cups plain flour
1 teaspoon cinnamon
1 cup butter

½ cup milk
6 slices canned pineapple, chopped
2 cups dates
2 cups cherries
7 cups pecans
1 teaspoon baking soda

Cream softened butter and sugar. Add eggs, baking soda and other ingredients. Drop by teaspoons onto greased cookie sheet. Bake 20 to 30 minutes at 375 degrees until just golden brown.

FRUIT DIP

Boil till thick:
⅓ cup cornstarch
½ cup sugar

1 quart milk

Add:
1 cup marshmallow cream

1 cup creamy peanut butter

Great with apple and banana chunks and pound cake.

FUDGE BROWNIES

Jennifer, Shirley's niece, loves this recipe. The only problem is she'll eat the batter before it hits the oven if you're not quick.

⅓ cup butter
1½ squares unsweetened chocolate
2 eggs
1 cup sugar
⅔ cup plain flour

½ teaspoon baking powder
¼ teaspoon salt
¾ cup walnuts, chopped
1 teaspoon vanilla extract

Melt butter and chocolate together in small double boiler or in saucepan over very low heat. Beat eggs until foamy, and gradually add sugar, beating well. Beat in chocolate mixture. Sift dry ingredients together and stir into batter until smooth. Next, stir in walnuts and vanilla. Pour into greased 8 x 8 x 2 inch pan. Bake at 350 degrees for 25 minutes.

MEMAW'S MERINGUE SHELLS

Memaw McCorvey was a wonderful cook.
This is a no fail way to cook meringue shells.

4 egg whites
1 cup sugar

1 teaspoon vanilla
1 teaspoon vinegar

Beat whites until stiff; add other ingredients and beat until shiny and very stiff. Draw circles on paper sacks and spread with spoon or pipe with pastry tube within confines of circles. Bake in 225 degree oven until brown. Turn oven off, leaving shells in oven until completely cool. May be cooked before hand and stored in airtight container until ready to use. At Rose Hill, we make them bite size and fill with custard topped with whipped cream and garnish with kiwi or fresh strawberry half.

PEACH CHARLOTTE

Shirley's nephew, Michael, loves this dessert! When she makes it at home, someone always comes up short because he's helped himself to more than his share. Rose Hill serves this at many of their ladies luncheons. It makes a lovely presentation.

6 egg yolks
1 cup sugar
2 cups milk
2 envelopes unflavored gelatin

½ cup cold milk
3 tablespoons sweet cream sherry
2 cups heavy cream, whipped

Peach Sauce:
3 cups peeled, pitted and sliced
    fresh peaches
½ cup sugar

2 tablespoons cornstarch
1 tablespoon peach schnapps
    (optional)

In top of double boiler over hot water, stir egg yolks, sugar and two cups milk using a wooden spoon. Soak gelatin in cold water until softened; add to hot custard. Stir until dissolved. Cook, stirring constantly until custard thickens. Remove from heat, cool and stir in sherry. Fold in whipped cream. Pour into stemmed glasses and chill. Top with peach sauce and a dollop of additional whipped cream.

Peach Sauce: Purée peaches in processor. Place purée, sugar and cornstarch in heavy saucepan. Cook over medium heat until sugar has dissolved and mixture thickens. Cool and add schnapps. Put about 2 tablespoons over Charlotte and dollop with whipped cream. Charlotte is very light and delicate. It's delicious served with whipped cream only.

CREAMY RICE PUDDING

Shirley's favorite!

2 cups cream
⅔ cup light brown sugar
½ teaspoon salt
1 teaspoon cinnamon

3 tablespoons butter
3 cups cooked white rice
½ cup raisins

Pecan Sauce:
1 cup light brown sugar
1 heaping tablespoon cornstarch
1 cup water

3 tablespoons butter
1 cup pecans
2 teaspoons vanilla extract

In saucepan, heat cream, brown sugar, salt, cinnamon and butter on low heat until sugar is dissolved. DO NOT boil. Remove from heat and stir cream mixture with rice and raisins. Pour into greased 9 x 13 inch baking dish. Place in larger pan with 1 inch deep water. Bake at 325 degrees for 30 minutes. Let cool 15 minutes before serving and top with pecan sauce and whipped cream. Serves 6 to 8.

Pecan Sauce: Brown butter on low heat and set aside. Mix sugar and cornstarch in saucepan. Stir in cold water and cook, stirring constantly, over low heat. Cook until clear. Remove from heat and add browned butter, pecans and vanilla. Let cool.

RICK'S PECAN SANDIES

*Shirley's brothers, Marty and Rick, are quite good cooks themselves.
This is a recipe Rick's friend, Beth Daniel, shared with him.
He is the "cookie master" of the family.*

2 cups plain flour
6 tablespoons sugar
2 sticks butter, softened

1½ cups pecans, chopped
2 teaspoons vanilla extract
powdered sugar

Cream butter and sugar with electric mixer. Add flour, pecans and vanilla extract and mix well. Roll by tablespoons into log shaped cookies. Bake on ungreased cookie sheet in preheated 350 degree oven for 15 to 20 minutes until golden brown. Cool and roll in powdered sugar. Cookies crisp up after they cool. They will melt in your mouth. Makes 4 to 5 dozen.

SUMMERTIME BLACKBERRY COBBLER

Shirley and her brothers, Marty and Rick use to wreck havoc in Dabbo's kitchen in the summer. Blackberry Cobbler was their favorite. Somehow Marty, the oldest, got the sweet end of the deal on this dish. He stayed home making the crust while Shirley and Rick drudged the woods for blackberries.

4 cups blackberries
2 cups plain flour
2 cups sugar

2 sticks butter, softened
juice of 1 lemon

Wash and drain berries. Put berries in a 2 quart buttered baking dish. Sprinkle with lemon juice. Mix all remaining ingredients with hands. Crumble over berries. Bake uncovered for 45 to 50 minutes in preheated 350 degree oven until crust is light brown. Serves 6 to 8.

CHOCOLATE PECAN PIE SQUARES

1 cup all-purpose flour
1/3 cup firmly packed dark brown
   sugar
3 tablespoons unsweetened cocoa
1 1/4 sticks butter (about 10
   tablespoons), cut into bits

1/4 cup dark corn syrup
2 large eggs
1/4 cup sugar
1/2 teaspoon vanilla
1 cup pecans, chopped

In food processor, blend flour, brown sugar, cocoa and 8 tablespoons butter until mixture resembles coarse meal. Press mixture into 8 x 8 inch pan and bake at 350 degrees for 10 to 15 minutes.

In a bowl whisk together the eggs, sugar, corn syrup, and remaining 2 tablespoons butter, melted. Add vanilla and pecans. Pour over baked chocolate crust and continue baking at 375 degrees for 20 to 25 minutes until filling is puffed and golden. Let cool. Cut into squares. Makes 16 squares.

CHOCOLATE-AMARETTO TARTS

1 1-ounce square unsweetened chocolate
½ cup butter, softened
2 cups powdered sugar
1 tablespoon vanilla extract (do not use imitation vanilla)
dash of salt

4 egg yolks
3 tablespoons Amaretto
1½ cups whipping cream
¼ cup sugar
1½ tablespoons Amaretto
Tart Shells (recipe follows)
toasted pecans (optional)

Melt chocolate in heavy saucepan over low heat; set aside.

Cream butter; gradually add powdered sugar, beating in mixer on medium speed until smooth. Add chocolate and blend well. Add vanilla and salt. Add egg yolks, one at a time, beating after each addition. Add 3 tablespoons Amaretto, 1 tablespoon at a time, beating well.

Beat whipping cream until soft peaks form. Gradually add 1½ tablespoons Amaretto and ¼ cup sugar; mix until blended. Fold 1 cup whipped mixture into chocolate mixture.

Fill cooled tart shells with chocolate filling. Chill 3 to 4 hours until firm. Dollop with reserved cream. Garnish with toasted pecans if desired.

Tart Shells:
66 vanilla wafers, divided
2 cups flaked coconut, divided

1 cup pecan pieces, divided
1 cup butter, melted

Crumble 33 vanilla wafers in container of food processor; add 1 cup coconut and ½ cup pecans and pulse 5 seconds. Repeat with remaining same ingredients. Pour melted butter over crumb mixture and toss lightly. Spoon 1 tablespoon crumb mixture into miniature muffin pans. Press to form crust on bottom and sides. Bake at 375 degrees for 8 to 10 minutes. Cool. Loosen tarts and fill them in the pan. Yield 5 dozen.

TEATIME TASSIES

Pastry Shells:

1 3-ounce package cream cheese   1 cup sifted plain flour
½ cup softened butter or
    margarine

Make pastry shells by combining cream cheese, butter or margarine, and flour. Chill about 1 hour then mold into mini muffin pans. Makes 24.

Filling:

1 egg   1 teaspoon vanilla
1 tablespoon soft butter or   dash salt
    margarine   ⅔ cup coarsely broken pecans

Beat together egg, sugar, butter or margarine, vanilla and salt until just smooth. Divide half the pecans among pastry lined cups; add egg mixture and top with remaining pecans. Bake in slow oven (325 degrees) 25 minutes or until set.

LEMON SQUARES

1 cup cake flour   2 tablespoons sugar
⅓ cup oleo   1¼ teaspoons salt

Blend flour, sugar, salt, and oleo with pastry blender. Press into greased pan. Bake at 300 degrees until golden brown.

2nd Layer:

1 cup brown sugar   ½ cup coconut
2 eggs, slightly beaten   ½ cup nuts (we use pecans)

Mix brown sugar, eggs, coconut, and nuts. Add this on top of first mixture while still hot. Put back in oven and bake until hard, about 20 to 25 minutes.

3rd Layer:

⅔ cup confectioner's sugar   grated lemon rind
2 tablespoons lemon juice

Mix confectioner's sugar, lemon juice and some grated lemon rind. When cake is cool, spread evenly over top. Cut into small squares. This is very rich. Can be frozen.

BLUEBERRY COFFEE CAKE

1¼ cups fresh blueberries
⅓ cup sugar
2 tablespoons cornstarch
½ cup butter, softened
1 cup sugar
2 eggs
2 cups plain flour

1 teaspoon baking powder
1 teaspoon soda
½ teaspoon salt
8 ounces sour cream
1 teaspoon almond extract
½ cup finely chopped pecans

Combine blueberries, ⅓ cup sugar and cornstarch in small saucepan. Cook over low heat for about 5 minutes, stirring constantly, until sauce is thickened. Set aside to cool. Cream butter. Gradually add 1 cup sugar beating until light and creamy. Add eggs 1 at a time beating well. Sift dry ingredients together. Add to creamed mixture in 4 parts alternately with sour cream in 3 parts; beginning and ending with flour. When alternating ingredients, beat on low speed just enough to mix in. Gently stir in extract. Spoon half of batter into a greased and floured tube pan. Spoon on half of blueberry mixture; slightly swirling through batter with a knife. Repeat with remaining batter and blueberries. Sprinkle with pecans. Bake in preheated 350 degree oven for 50 to 60 minutes. Let stand 5 minutes; remove from pan. Drizzle with glaze.

Glaze: Combine ¾ cup sifted powdered sugar, 1 tablespoon milk and ½ teaspoon almond extract. Whisk until smooth. Double glaze recipe if heavier glaze is desired.

CHEESE DAINTIES

We have served these easily prepared pick-up desserts for many occasions.

8 ounces cream cheese
2 eggs
1 cup confectioner's sugar

1 teaspoon vanilla, or your
favorite extract

Cream cheese and eggs. Add sugar and vanilla. Spoon into small muffin tins that have been prepared with liquid non-stick spray. Bake at 325 degrees 25 minutes. DO NOT brown. Top with whipped cream and sliced fruit garnish. Serves 12.

SWEET CHEESE DAINTIES

Here is a different version.

Pastry Cups:
2 cups plain flour
2 sticks butter, softened

1 8-ounce package cream cheese, softened

Cheese Filling:
1 8-ounce package softened cream cheese
1 egg
½ cup sugar

1 teaspoon vanilla extract, or orange
1 teaspoon grated lemon or orange rind

Pastry: Blend all together. Refrigerate for 30 minutes. Pinch off and roll into rounds. Mold into mini-muffin tins.

Cheese Filling: Combine all ingredients; beat at medium speed of electric mixer or pulse till blended. Fill prepared pastry cups. Bake at 375 degrees for 20 to 25 minutes. Remove from pan and cool on wire rack. If desired, dust with powdered sugar before serving. Yield 3½ dozen.

MABLE HINDS' TEA CAKES

Mable Hinds is in Barbara's Mother's (MA) Sunday school class at the Highland Gardens Baptist Church. Ma is a charter member of the church. Everytime they have an event that includes refreshments, Mable has to bring her tea cakes. They are melt in your mouth good. They sort of remind us of Scottish short bread.

1 cup butter, softened
1 cup Crisco
2 cups sugar
6 cups plain flour

1 teaspoon salt
2 teaspoons soda
2 eggs

Cream butter, Crisco and sugar until sugar is incorporated. Add flour mixed with salt and soda. Add eggs and stir until just mixed. Roll out on floured surface and cut into cookies. Bake at 350 degrees until just lightly browned. Will firm as they cool.

Note: This batter freezes well. Ma rolls it into logs, wraps it in wax paper, puts it into zip locks and freezes. Then she just cuts the rolls with a knife into the thickness she wants.

RUM BALLS

1 6-ounce package semisweet
    chocolate pieces
½ cup sugar
⅓ cup rum
3 tablespoons light corn syrup

2 cups crushed vanilla wafers (44
    wafers)
1 cup ground walnuts
sugar

In a saucepan, melt chocolate over low heat. Remove from heat, and stir in
½ cup sugar, rum, and corn syrup. Fold in nuts and crushed wafers. Shape
mixture into 1 inch balls, using about 2 teaspoons for each ball. Roll in sugar,
and store in an air tight container for several days before serving. Makes
about 4 dozen.

GRAHAM CRACKER GOODIES

This is very quick and easy. Young people especially enjoy this.

honey graham crackers
1½ sticks butter
¼ cup sugar

1 teaspoon vanilla
½ cup chopped nuts

Line cookie sheet with graham crackers. Boil butter, sugar and vanilla until
blended. Add chopped nuts. Spread on top of graham crackers. Bake at 400
degrees for 8 minutes. Take up while hot. Cool then break apart.

APPLEJACK CUSTARD SAUCE

This recipe is great over poached pears, peaches or apples.

2 cups milk
½ cup sugar
8 large egg yolks

½ teaspoon vanilla extract
pinch salt
¼ cup Applejack liqueur

Bring milk and ¼ cup sugar to boil in medium saucepan, stirring until sugar
dissolves. Whisk remaining ¼ cup sugar, yolks, vanilla and salt in small bowl.
Gradually whisk ½ of milk mixture into yolks. Return mixture to saucepan
and stir until custard thickens; do not boil. Strain into bowl. Refrigerate till
cool. Mix in applejack. Cover and refrigerate till cold. Yield 3 cups.

ORANGE BUTTERMILK CUSTARD PUDDING

We use buttermilk in many of our recipes at Panache at Rose Hill. Remember, buttermilk was a staple in the rural South, so our grandmothers became very creative in its use. Here's a twist to an old favorite.

¾ cup sugar	3 eggs, separated
3 tablespoons cornstarch	1½ teaspoons orange or lemon zest
1½ cups buttermilk (remember to shake well before pouring)	¼ cup orange or lemon juice
	¼ cup sugar
2 tablespoons butter	¼ teaspoon cream of tartar

Over low heat, cook together sugar and cornstarch, stirring constantly. Add buttermilk stirring till thick. Add butter. Combine egg yolks, rind and juice. Stir small bit of hot mixture into yolks, then add to remaining hot mixture. Continue stirring. Cook till smooth and thickened. Pour into 4 ungreased custard cups. Hollowed orange halves or lemon cups may be used in lieu of custard cups.

Beat egg whites on high speed till foamy. Add sugar and cream of tartar, beating until stiff peaks form. Spread meringue over custards, sealing edges. Bake at 375 degrees for 2 to 5 minutes until lightly browned. Cool before serving. Makes 4 servings.

HARD SAUCE

⅓ cup butter	1 teaspoon vanilla, lemon or
1 cup confectioners' sugar	orange extract
1 tablespoon whipping cream	lemon or orange zest

Cream butter until soft; add sugar, beating well. Add cream and extract, beating until fluffy. Brandy, rum or sherry may be substituted for cream and flavoring. Great over fried pies. Yield ¾ cup.

RICE PUDDING WITH CURRANT JELLY AND LEMON SAUCE

Rice was also a staple in the rural South. We use many rice recipes at the restaurant. Shirley has her favorite rice pudding; this is mine.

⅔ cup long-grain rice
3 cups milk
peel of 1 lemon
1 cup sugar
2 tablespoons lemon juice

2 tablespoons butter
¼ teaspoon salt
4 eggs, separated
6 tablespoons red currant jelly, heated

Sauce:
½ cup sugar
¼ teaspoon salt
1 tablespoon cornstarch
1 cup water

2 teaspoons grated lemon peel
3 tablespoons lemon juice
3 tablespoons butter

Rinse rice. Cook in milk in double boiler about 30 minutes. Pulse lemon peel and ½ cup sugar in processor until peel is finely grated. Add peeling mixture lemon juice, salt and egg yolks (beaten) to cooked rice. Pour into prepared 1½ quart baking dish. Bake at 350 degrees about 30 minutes until knife inserted comes out not quite clear. (It will continue to set while it cools). Cool 10 to 15 minutes. Spoon jelly on top. Beat egg whites till foamy. Add ½ cup sugar and beat till stiff. Spread over pudding. Bake at 400 degrees 10 to 15 minutes till brown. Serve with lemon sauce. Serves 6.

Sauce: Combine sugar, salt and cornstarch in saucepan. Stir in water and bring to a boil. Cook till thick and clear, 5 to 6 minutes. Remove from heat. Add peel and juice. Blend in butter. Serve over pudding.

INDEX

B

C

T

V

B.J. INVESTMENTS, INC.
11250 HWY. 80, E
MONTGOMERY, AL 36117

Please send _____ copy(ies) of

Panache at Rose Hill @ $14.95   each _____

Postage and handling @   3.00   each _____

Alabama residents add sales tax .06% @   .90   each _____

Total _____

Name _____

Address _____

City _____ State _____ Zip _____

Make checks payable to B. J. Investments, Inc.

B.J. INVESTMENTS, INC.
11250 HWY. 80, E
MONTGOMERY, AL 36117

Please send _____ copy(ies) of

Panache at Rose Hill @ $14.95   each _____

Postage and handling @   3.00   each _____

Alabama residents add sales tax .06% @   .90   each _____

Total _____

Name _____

Address _____

City _____ State _____ Zip _____

Make checks payable to B. J. Investments, Inc.

B.J. INVESTMENTS, INC.
11250 HWY. 80, E
MONTGOMERY, AL 36117

Please send _____ copy(ies) of

Panache at Rose Hill @ $14.95   each _____

Postage and handling @   3.00   each _____

Alabama residents add sales tax .06% @   .90   each _____

Total _____

Name _____

Address _____

City _____ State _____ Zip _____

Make checks payable to B. J. Investments, Inc.